Teach with Magic

Use Disney Design Techniques to Make Your Classroom the Most Engaging Place on Earth!

Kevin Roughton

Theme Park Press
The Happiest Books on Earth
www.ThemeParkPress.com

Editor: Bob McLain
Layout: Artisanal Text

ISBN 978-1-68390-306-2
Printed in the United States of America

Theme Park Press | www.ThemeParkPress.com
Address queries to bob@themeparkpress.com

Contents

A Note to the Reader

This book is a collection of my thoughts on teaching tied directly to my experiences with Disney, and particularly those of Disney Imagineering's design principles outlined in Marty Sklar's *One Little Spark: Mickey's 10 Commandments and the Road to Imagineering*. It is, at times, autobiographical but always personal. If I write about it, I did it! Every lesson and activity comes from my classroom. This is real stuff, not theory!

I wrote the first draft of this book in the Before-Times, before the COVID-19 pandemic of 2020 changed so much about education. You'll see that my references seem to be from another time. That's because they are. I considered major rewrites or adding an additional chapter. However, I believe that we will see those seemingly quaint times again. It may take a while, but someday we'll be giving high-fives again. Additionally, I believe that the spirit behind my examples are still alive. Even if you are social distancing or fully online with your teaching, providing a magical experience to our students is still key.

Additional writings of mine about teaching can be found on the *Let's Teach with Magic* blog found at www.teachwithmagic. com. You will also find archives of my conference presentations, technical tutorials on some of the techniques in the book and all my lessons and activities. I've also shared many of my distance learning lessons there and on my Twitter page at https://twitter.com/MrRoughton. Every lesson and activity I've created and used with my students are free for other teachers to use with their students. Yes, free. Please take them. Use them. Adapt them. We're in this together!

This book is not endorsed by nor affiliated or associated with Disney or the Disney corporation. No harm is intended toward any of their property, copyrights, or trademarks. All historical information presented is believed to be accurate based on my personal research. While there are often conflicting versions of how certain events played out in Disney history, I believe I have represented them truthfully and, at the very least, in the correct spirit. I have tried to maintain the Disney spirit throughout. In that vein, I often refer to Disney employees using their first name. That is not to imply I had a relationship with those people, it is simply a continuance of a policy put into place by Walt Disney himself.

I hope you will enjoy sharing my memories and experiences of Disneyland and, more importantly, come away with ideas that help to make your classroom the most engaging place on Earth for your students.

Let's teach with magic!

Introduction

On July 16, 2019 I woke up at 5:45 AM for a yet another trip to Disneyland. This time my mom and I were taking my young cousin, Nathan, for his 8th birthday. He hadn't been to the park since he was three and had only the vaguest memories of it. We arrived to pick him up at 7:02 AM. He was already waiting outside with his backpack on. We pulled into the driveway and he jumped up out of his chair exclaiming, "THEY'RE HERE!"

Nathan's excitement didn't diminish an ounce over the next 12 hours. He chattered away throughout the hour-long drive and squealed with delight when he saw our parking lot tram painted with *Toy Story* characters. He marveled at each window display he passed, repeatedly saying with exasperation, "Oh no!" as in, "Oh no! How could this amazing thing actually exist?!" At every opportunity he sat up and as close to the action as possible, leading our Jungle Cruise Skipper (who was also standing) to tell him "only someone crazy would stand on a boat!" He talked to anyone who would listen about anything he could think of. He loved every second of it.

What is it about Disneyland?

When you're there somehow the world is a better place. People are happy, friendly and (mostly) patient. The most hardened looking adult can be found wearing felt ears, singing along with costumed characters and dancing down the streets. Strollers worth hundreds of dollars are left parked without supervision. People leave their backpacks and merchandise bags sitting right out in the open with no fear that the tens of thousands of other guests, whom they've likely never met, will take them. You are so wrapped up in the magic that you don't even consider it. Disneyland isn't just the happiest place on Earth, it's the most engaging place on Earth! This isn't the usual world where people are on the defensive all the time. This is a magical world that we all agree to live in for at least a little while when we walk through the gates, and that is by design. As Imagineer John Hench put it, "We give power to the guests' imagination, to transcend their everyday routine."

A Disney fan in the YouTube comments of the audio track to the Paint the Night parade explained it from the guest perspective. "People who have never been to Disney Land won't understand the magic of it and how sad you get afterward because you just want to stay forever!!! it makes you feel like a little kid again! it's like something sparks inside of you because you are sooooo happy. heaven on earth. I was litterally breaking down when I left Disney Land. it's like it's leaving everything you love." [sic] -Quinn Patryce, *YouTube* Comments

That's what I want out of my classroom.

No, that's what I want out of *every* classroom.

Engagement has always been important to learning, but I'd argue now more so than ever. Like just about everything else in the last 15 years, education has changed dramatically thanks to the Internet and modern technology. Our students now carry in their pockets access to more information than they ever had in a set of textbooks or encyclopedias. Siri and Alexa know more than you or I ever could. Those same devices provide on-demand entertainment of any type imaginable. That is our competition. An engaged brain is a learning brain and with information and entertainment so ubiquitous much of our information delivery is going to come up short in really reaching our students. While information delivery still has a place in our classrooms what we truly need to offer to our students are experiences that build on that information. We need to engage those brains!

And nobody delivers exciting, memorable, engaging experiences like Disney.

Hundreds of books have been written about the magic of Disney. There are dozens about Walt Disney, even more about Disneyland and Disney World, and plenty examining the company's customer service and business practices. Far fewer, however, have been written about the wizards behind the magic, the Imagineers, and in particular, the man who served as their president, heart and soul for many years, Marty Sklar.

This branch of the company has traditionally been kept in greater secrecy than the rest. A magician never gives away his secrets, right? In the beginning, this secretive branch that is today known as Walt Disney Imagineering was not even part of the Walt Disney Company that owned the movie studio and theme park. Walt held on tight to his creative arm keeping it as a separate company, far away from the finance side of the Disney business. Walt (using words written by Marty Sklar) defined Imagineering as "the blending of creative imagination with technical know-how." The Imagineers who worked in this division were responsible for designing and building Walt's dream theme park. Many of the first Imagineers were artists with film experience. They brought a unique vision of the importance of story, color and visual design to designing the park.

Imagineers are responsible for nearly everything one experiences at Disney parks. They design the attractions, stores, restaurants, streets, costumes and even the trash cans! They are responsible for the colors you see, the sounds you hear and the odors you smell. For decades, the ways of Imagineering were kept secret. Disney did not want their competition stealing their ideas or, perhaps more importantly, their talent!

In recent years, Disney has recognized there is a hunger among fans to learn more about these people who create the incredible experiences we love. In 2019 they released *The Imagineering Story*, a 6-part documentary series that traces the history of Disney parks through the eyes of the Imagineers who built them. They've also published a couple of beautiful coffee-table books about Imagineering and many former Imagineers like Marc Davis and Kevin Rafferty have written books chronicling their own journeys to and through Imagineering.

My personal favorite of these books, and the one sent me down this rabbit hole into researching Imagineering history, is Marty Sklar's *One Little Spark: Mickey's Ten Commandments and the Road to Imagineering*. It outlines the design principles the Imagineers follow to create their amazing attractions.

If anyone had the right to write such a thing, other than Walt Disney, it was Marty Sklar. He was, almost literally, Walt's mouthpiece for years, serving as his chief speech writer. He is the only Disney cast member to be a part of the opening of every Disney park around the world from Anaheim to Shanghai. After starting as a writer for *The Disneyland News* at Disneyland he worked his way up the ladder at the company. Eventually, he served as the creative director for Disney Imagineering before ultimately becoming president. During that time he supervised the construction of eight Disney parks around the world. His final years with the company were as an Imagineering Ambassador where he traveled the world giving talks about the magic of Imagineering. In his book *Magic Journey,* Imagineer Kevin Rafferty says of Marty, "He was a force, the force, at WED (the early name for Imagineering), and if he wasn't on the move in our hallowed hallways or on the road for research at a project or construction site, he was out wheeling and dealing and schmoozing with potential or existing corporate alliance partners." So, if one wants to learn about how Imagineering works it makes sense to hear it from Marty.

In the last few years, I've had the opportunity to meet people ranging from teachers to Imagineers who knew and worked with Marty. Every single one of them lit up when talking about him. Marty was a great mentor, as all great teachers are. Rafferty added in Marty's own *Travels with Figment,* published after his passing, "We could not have asked for a better boss, mentor, teacher, advocate and dear and cherished friend." His window on Main Street, U.S.A. in Disneyland honoring his service recognizes him as the "Dean of the College of Arts and Sciences." He is a far-too-unsung hero in the Disney story. While it would have been great to meet Walt Disney, I really wish I'd had the opportunity to meet Marty. His words in *One Little Spark* have truly inspired me as an educator and my intent with this book is to help fellow educators learn from his wisdom.

* * *

So, why me? In what way am I possibly qualified to write a book with the ridiculously lofty goal of turning every classroom into Disneyland?

First, I'm a teacher, not a former one. Any time I present at a conference I see presenters with fancy titles like "Educational Consultant" or "Learning Representative." At first it was intimidating. I felt wildly underqualified. However, many of my audience members commented that they appreciated my honesty and willingness to say, "I don't know." My vulnerability came from being a teacher. One simply cannot give five performances a day to an audience of twelve-year-olds without learning some humility! Now when I present I'm honored to list my title as "Just a Teacher!" I'm in the trenches every day. I've taught middle school in a low income, high minority, Title I school that is just a few minutes from my house for over 15 years. Every word I write in this book comes from experience, both good and bad. Theory is fun to talk about but actually putting things into practice is so much more important. I've done that for years, and I've done it well. I was recognized as the 2016 Outstanding Middle Level Educator by the California Council for the Social Studies and as 2017's Outstanding Teacher of American History in California by the Daughters of the American Revolution. I'm good at being "just a teacher!"

I've shared all my lessons and creations on my personal website for years. I've had people contact me from all around the world saying they've used a lesson or two of mine and loved the experience. That has given me the opportunity to present at multiple conferences around Southern California and even serve as the keynote speaker a couple times. Often after presenting an attendee would say, "You should write a book on this stuff." Seed planted. Then, while attending a conference for educators at Disneyland hosted by the Imagineers an attendee told them, "Someone should write a book about this so other educators can hear it too." Well, okay, if you insist!

While I'm proud of my qualifications as a teacher they don't stack up to my qualifications as a voice on Disney.

You see, I don't like to brag but my name is literally etched on a brick outside of Disneyland. My name is part of the foundation of Disneyland! What more proof could you need?! They don't just let anyone put their names on those bricks you see. You have to pay good money for it! (Or, your parents do as a graduation gift but that's just semantics.)

If somehow that incredible achievement doesn't convince you, I've also read pretty much every book in existence about Disney Imagineering, I have visited Disneyland well over 100 times in my life, I can recite all of the Haunted Mansion soundtrack, I've made it to the 500,000 point question in Who Wants to be a Millionaire: Play it!, I've eaten at Club 33, I've been in Walt Disney's apartment... AND my name is etched in a brick outside Disneyland!

There, certified Disney nerd... I mean fan.

So I, Mr. Roughton, "just a teacher" and huge Disneyland fan will be your guide through Mickey's 10 Commandments. We'll explore how these magical rules drive the creation of Disneyland's incredible attractions and how we can recreate those experiences in our own classrooms. As a historian I hope you'll enjoy the stories of Disneyland and Imagineering history along with my own personal reflections and experiences as we take this journey together.

And know this is a journey well worth taking. I'd argue the skill most valued at Imagineering is creativity. It is pretty much what they do. I think we educators fail to recognize how important that skill is for us. Creativity is rarely discussed among teachers. It often only comes up when someone shares a picture they found on Pinterest of some impossibly perfect classroom. The response is often, "I wish I were that creative!" That is usually the end of it. We assume creativity is a genetic trait and we just didn't get it like that teacher must have.

This feeling is really not our fault. We go through teacher training programs where often the only thing we are taught about creating lessons is that they have to follow a very structured format that checks off all the boxes.

Objective? Check.

Anticipatory set? Check.

Guided Instruction? Check.

Independent practice? Check.

Check for understanding? Check.

I've got a lesson!

There's not a whole lot of room for creativity in that checklist and certainly not a requirement for it. I mean come on, there's not even a check box for it!

What if instead we had other questions?
What will my students experience?
What will my students enjoy?
What will my students remember?

These were not questions I was asked to consider in my teacher education program in 2002 and, based on what I've heard from my student teachers over the last 15 years, they still largely are not. Some programs are getting better about it but creativity is just not an expectation for prospective teachers. As a result, we don't teach how to do it. Also, creativity is often presented as an innate talent that you either have or don't, but creativity *can* be taught, or at least guided. That's where Mickey's 10 commandments come in!

1. Know your audience
2. Wear your guests' shoes
3. Organize the flow of people and ideas
4. Create a wienie (visual magnet)
5. Communicate with visual literacy
6. Avoid overload, create turn-ons
7. Tell one story at a time
8. Avoid contradictions
9. For every ounce of treatment, add a ton of treat
10. Keep it up! (Maintain it)

This list, written by Marty Sklar, was developed based on his years of experience as creative lead and president at Imagineering. These "commandments" have guided the most creative people on Earth, surely they can work for us too!

Teaching isn't a formula, and you *are* creative! You are creative every time you have to adjust a lesson to reach that one student who just isn't getting it. You are creative every time you seek to modify an unwanted behavior with new discipline techniques. We are constantly thinking on our feet and making adjustments as teachers. That's creativity! It just doesn't fit the traditional mold of it, so we don't see it.

What if we applied that creativity to our lessons? Could we create incredible learning experiences for our students? Could we make our classrooms a place they want to be, not just a place they have to be? Could we design an engaging environment that welcomes our students and leaves their senses all so fulfilled that remembering the day's learning is a joy not a challenge?

As Rafferty, who was head designer of the masterpiece Cars Land at Disney California Adventure, put it, "If you can create an attraction that keeps guests in its spell, that's the art and magic of Imagineering." That is my goal for my classroom. To create learning experiences so engaging that students are living them. I don't want them to pretend to be historians. I want them to *be* historians! I want our classrooms to be Disneyland; a place where students are eager to enter and loath to leave. With guidance from the Imagineers and Mickey's 10 commandments, they can be.

My goal with this book is to be inspirational and aspirational. In each chapter I'll take you along on a trip through my memories of Disneyland. I'll share examples from the parks of the commandments in action. Then, I'll show you how those commandments work in my classroom and might in yours. In some cases I'll provide step by step instructions but, in many cases, I'm going to leave it to you to learn the practical steps. I am a firm believer that any educator can learn to do anything I share in this book. You don't need me to tell you every little step. You are a professional learner, you've got this!

Let's teach with magic!

CHAPTER ONE

Know Your Audience

"Identify the prime audience for your attraction or show."

-Marty Sklar, *Dream It, Do It!*

One morning, early in the school year, I sat at my computer in the precious few I-can-breathe-the-students-aren't-here-yet minutes, scrolling through my list of music. Not quite awake enough for *Rage Against the Machine*. Not willing to risk a colleague hearing *Savage Garden*. Ah. This is the one...

> *The Battle of Yorktown, 1781.*
> *Monsieur Hamilton!*
> *Monsieur Lafayette!*

Yes, the *Hamilton* soundtrack will do just fine.

Valerie walked in and with the sound of excited surprise you can truly only get from a middle school girl, somehow asked and exclaimed at the same time, "Is this *Hamilton*?!" "Yep." Bonding complete. Valerie and I ended up having many Hamilton-centered conversations in those before school minutes over the remainder of the year. Through them I learned she'd been involved in theater since she was 3. She repeatedly told me about writing and directing our school play, the first we'd had in 20 years. I made sure to attend and asked her to autograph my ticket after the show. She giggled as she asked, "Why?" I replied, "So someday when your name is in lights I can sell it and retire!"

That summer I went on a tour of the Hyperion Theater at Disney California Adventure where Frozen Live is performed. The stage manager of the show led us backstage. I saw the puppets worth tens of thousands of dollars and the cutting-edge technology likely worth many times more. Throughout I thought, "Val would love this. I can't wait to tell her about it!" At the very end our guide told us that if we had any students interested in theater, she'd be happy to have them come for a tour. She said they could even possibly sit in the booth with her for a performance. Well, I guess I didn't have to just tell Val about it.

I called her parents in the middle of the summer. I was pretty sure they had annual passes. Valerie was regularly absent from class. I'd ask her why and, more than once, the answer was "I was up late at Disneyland." Sounds like a fellow passholder to me! I told Valerie's mom about the opportunity after she confirmed my suspicions were correct. The tone in her voice made it clear she was elated at the idea. She thanked me and said, "Valerie got so excited when she heard it was you on the phone. She knew it had to be something great!"

A few weeks later, on the same July 16th that I visited the parks with my cousin, I sat on the curb outside the Hyperion Theater, mostly enjoying my Strawberry Banana Sensation smoothie (the Berry Schmoozie is better it turns out) in an attempt to mitigate the mid-summer California sun. I was unsuccessful. Thankfully, just a few minutes later, Valerie and her family appeared walking down Hollywood Boulevard and the sun quickly left my mind. We chatted for a while outside the theater before Valerie's mom asked, "You're coming in with us, right?" How could I say no? The cast member at the front directed us to the VIP waiting area right at the entrance to the theater. Valerie's motor was running at a mile a minute, not unlike my 8-year-old cousin. It was a joy to behold.

As VIPs we were let in first and given priority seating. Valerie joined the stage manager in the booth as promised. She was given a headset and the opportunity to listen in to all the director's chatter throughout the show. Just before show-time Valerie's mom looked over at her dad and asked, with a smile, "Why are you crying?" He replied back, "Why are YOU crying?!" I jumped in to ask, "Why am I crying?!" All of us had a tear in our eye seeing Valerie in her element. Throughout the show I couldn't stop myself from turning around to see Val wearing her headset. After the show we all went backstage like I had done on my "exclusive" tour earlier that summer. That is a magical moment! It was a joy for Valerie, but it was just as joyful for all of us involved in making it happen. I know one day when Valerie's name is in lights she'll think back to this experience and remember how it pushed her further on her path.

It truly was a magical moment and now I'm one step closer to retiring off of that autograph!

* * *

When we get to know our kids, we can form relationships that open doors to amazing experiences in our classrooms. While surely not all of them will be like the one I got to have with Valerie, smaller ones can happen every day. From a student pouring their heart out over struggles at home to sharing a quick laugh over a silly joke, these experiences build connections and make teaching not just easier, but far more enjoyable.

That's why one of my favorite "teacherisms" is answering the question "What do you teach?" with "Kids." While I truly believe content is important, recognizing that we are teaching that content to a specific audience is sometimes lost in our profession. I believe the best teachers are those that can teach any content because they are actually just teaching kids. Knowing kids is much harder than knowing content. If you can do the former, I trust you can figure out the latter as well. Know for whom you are designing your experiences!

Knowing our audience can seem like an impossible task. As a secondary teacher I have at least 120 different students every year. I have 160ish days with each of them once we remove the days they or I are out of class. In each of those days I only see a given student for an hour (or two if I'm lucky enough to have them in my elective class.) That hour is packed full of content. My classroom runs from bell to bell. I've got standards to teach! I'm not unique in that. If anything, I've got it easy. Some of you have far more students and far more intense testing requirements. Impossible.

Or is it?

When Walt Disney first imagined Disneyland he envisioned a park unlike any that existed prior. Plenty of parks existed for children, and adults had their entertainment venues as well, but few were designed for entire families. Walt's audience was not kids and adults separately, but families together. Now, Disneyland gets millions of visitors every year, tens of thousands every day, and they get far less time with their guests than we do with our students. On the day I show up at the gate at Disneyland the cast members (Disney speak for employees) don't know if I had breakfast that morning, if someone in my family is sick or if I'm having issues at work. They are never going to know my personal story. Yet, when I go to Disneyland, I feel like I'm home. I feel like I matter. They may not know me personally, but they know people. They know their audience. And we can too, even if we can't know every detail.

Thinking back to Valerie, I realize there's a ton about her I still don't know. I can't name a single song or artist she likes outside of Lin-Manuel Miranda. I don't know what foods she likes. I didn't even know she had a sister until I met her at Disneyland! I didn't need to know everything though. I knew, generally, what kids want and need from a teacher. I have a pretty good general understanding of 12-year-olds after teaching them for 18 years. From there I learned a few small things that were important to her specifically. That was all I needed to make a real connection with her, opening the door to provide her with the experience of a lifetime. This is a key lesson in knowing our audience. While our audience knowledge needs to go far deeper than "the collection of students sitting in my classroom," it doesn't mean we have to know every detail of every student. Just connecting with a student on one single thing can go a long way. If our students are just faces in the crowd they, and we, are not going to feel connected.

If you're wondering if you know your audience, consider these questions. Are you teaching this year's students the same way you did last year's? Do you teach all of your periods the same way? Do you know what interests drive your students? Do you know what sparks their curiosity? If your answers to these are no, then maybe it's time to do some guest research! I wish I could provide you these answers, but your audience is surely different from mine. My own audience, every year, is slightly different. I do my best to design with each particular audience in mind.

Knowing our audience means:

- knowing their challenges
- knowing their achievement levels
- knowing their abilities and skills
- knowing their interests
- knowing their dreams

My students, on average, from year to year are roughly the same in terms of abilities, interests and levels. I can expect, in any given class, to have some high achievers and some low ones. Some kids will go above and beyond on everything while others barely manage to turn anything in. I know what things they find funny and what assignments they really get into. While each year I have different individual audience members and different trends come and go, I feel like overall I know my audience pretty well. I make it a priority to do so. It helps that I'm a kid at heart so I love video games, cartoons and comic book movies. (I cannot however bring myself to have any interest in anyone called a "Youtuber" or pretty much any pop music that isn't in a Disney movie!) With that in mind, what do we know about our audience?

Our Audience

1. They want to feel loved and appreciated.

This one is easy. *Everyone* wants to feel loved and appreciated. Here is another specific spot where we can learn from Disney. Cast members are trained to bring joy to the guests whenever possible and make them feel at home, even when they don't know them personally. They are to treat the guests as if they are family. Years ago, I took a private tour at Disneyland where we were given name tags. Our tour guide, Nicole, addressed us by name multiple times throughout the two-hour adventure. It was immediately noticeable. I instantly felt comfortable talking to her and asking questions. At the end of the tour we stuck around and talked with her for about 20 minutes. Where we might have otherwise felt rushed or uncomfortable talking with a near stranger, her use of our names made us feel at home. This is an easy thing we can remember in our classrooms. Learning student names and using them early and often is a great way to show them they matter.

Unfortunately, this has been an area where I've long struggled. I'm so focused on getting my class going at the start of the year that learning names gets lost in the shuffle. Plus, it's hard! I have 150ish new kids every year and they are all roughly the same size and wearing the same style of clothes. In my 17th year of struggling with this I made a commitment to learn the names of at least my homeroom kids as soon as possible. I figured I could have them memorized after our first couple days and then work on a second class. Then I realized I didn't have to wait to meet them. Our attendance system includes student photos! I started memorizing their names the week before our school preview day, the day before the First Day. When they came to meet me, I greeted them by name. There were a few I couldn't quite remember (kids change a bit over a full year of 6th grade!), but I knew the majority. They were all stunned. Many asked how I knew their names already. I told them they would be my new family and families call each other by name. I felt more of a connection with those kids from day one than any others from my past years. Next year, I'll try to have two classes memorized!

It goes far beyond just names though. When you go to Disneyland, you can visit an information booth and receive a button to commemorate your day. You'll see people around the park wearing "It's my Birthday!" or "First Visit!" buttons. When Cast Members see those buttons, particularly the birthday one, they must acknowledge it. They are trained to stop and say happy birthday to the person with the button. When was the last time you sang happy birthday to a student? It's a small thing indeed, but Walt Disney understood the innate human desire to be valued and appreciated. Former Vice President of Walt Disney World Lee Cockerell in his excellent book on leadership, *Creating Magic*, put it this way; "all everyone wants is to feel special, to be treated with respect and to be seen as an individual."

I've tried to make that my goal, especially early in the year in my classroom. One of my students in 2019, Sara, said this about her feelings being in my class:

I've always appreciated your encouragement to me and others. You made me love something I never knew I could be somewhat good in. I want to learn more about everything from the Romans to the Pirates because of you. I don't know if you realized it, but you really helped me bring my self-esteem up. From the smallest things, like saying I did a great job, they meant a lot to me even though I don't show it. I think it was the letter that you sent that really made me realize that I was worth something. I really had fun this year and I had an amazing year in your classroom. Thank you for caring and giving me a fantastic experience.

Sara is a special case, but not necessarily a unique one. She is naturally gifted and started the year off strong. She was my top performing student the first six weeks of school. Unfortunately, middle school caught up to her and she struggled to live up to her own expectations of perfection and quickly started missing due dates and fell behind on her work. She was still kind, participated in class discussions and never once was a behavior problem. By all outward appearances she was doing great. However, as another student, Giselle, reminded me recently, "just because I'm a good kid, it doesn't mean I don't struggle." I saw in Sara a young lady trying to find her place. She was striving for perfection, seeking that confidence they all want so badly. When given time to really put her all into something she created amazing work. That's really all I ever told her. I wrote a few very short notes on a couple of her tests like "Amazing, as always." and once wrote "I love it!" on one of her projects. I really didn't do much. In fact, I don't even remember sending her the letter! It is something we do as a staff at each staff meeting. We fill in a short postcard for a student that is mailed home. It took maybe 30 seconds of my time, but clearly meant the world to Sara. Our students really do just want to be valued!

This too is reflected in Disney practices. Cast members are not allowed to say, "I don't know." when asked a question. "I don't know." is giving up and implying that the guest isn't worth the time and effort. As a paying guest that is an insult. It makes you far less likely to want to come again and spend another small fortune. Instead, they at least have to say, "I'll find out." Guests want to feel valued, just like our students. I think we far too often shuffle them along to the next thing without stopping to make sure they feel like they matter.

Marty Sklar was great at doing this with his team at Imagineering, which is almost certainly why he seems to be universally loved. One of my favorite stories about Marty is one that he admits he isn't proud of. In his autobiography *Dream It, Do It!* he recounts a time he felt he had to stand up for his team. After one of their proposals was put down by a senior Disney executive as naive, he stood up to him, first cursing at him and then powerfully stating "and don't ever play the 'young man' game with my team again!" In doing so I have no doubt he engendered deep loyalty among his team. We can do the same for our kids. Know that they want to be loved and defended. Be their advocate!

Disney cast members are also encouraged to provide "magic moments" for guests by making decisions, even ones that may cost some money, in order to ensure a fantastic guest experience. It can be as simple as bringing a new ice cream to a child who dropped theirs, but these moments require the cast to be aware of the needs of their guests. In 2019 I went to see one of the final performances of the Main Street Electrical Parade. Guests lined up as early as 3 hours before the show to get a good view. As the parade began a Disney cast member appeared next to me with a young girl, 4 or 5 years old, holding her hand. The little girl was dressed as a princess and could not see from her spot many rows back. The cast member gave her a chance to experience the magic. The girl beamed with joy the entire time. She waved at every float or character who passed by, not stopping for the 15-minute duration of the show. The cast member, who was stuck kneeling very uncomfortably to avoid blocking other guests said to a colleague at the end, "man that hurt, but man was it worth it!" She got to provide that young girl with an experience she and her family will treasure forever. She knew her audience well. She knew first that the little girl would love the experience, but she also knew that the rest of the guests would understand why this girl was getting special treatment.

Think about how magical your classroom can be if you seek to know your audience so well that you can provide them with magic moments. I have my AVID kids write 10 paragraph autobiographies in their 8th grade year. AVID is an elective designed to prepare underserved students for college. This writing assignment forces them to go deeper into telling their life story than most ever have. In 2016, my student April wrote in hers that she had never had a birthday party of her own. She had a birthday very close to one of her cousins and they always shared a party. That little comment really drove home to me how much our audience wants to be recognized and appreciated. If April was driven to write about it then it had to be something that mattered to her. I made a mental note of the comment and waited for February to come around.

On April's birthday I threw her a party. I bought her a wand and a tiara from the dollar store. I bought a bunch of *One Direction* themed party favors and a copy of *Girl Talk: One Direction Edition* as her gift. (She also noted her love for *One Direction* in the same autobiography.) April sat on the chair in front of our AVID class, put on her tiara and was the princess for the day. After we sang for her and she opened her gift we played her new game together as a class. I played as well, of course. It got even better when the principal walked in for a random visit!

The whole experience was, quite simply, magical. April was overjoyed the whole time, but so was the rest of the class. This moment bonded that particular class in a powerful way.

It turns out one doesn't have to be the focus of a magical moment to enjoy the experience! Just like the crowd at the parade got to be a part of the young girl's magical experience, the other students in class shared April's experience and were further encouraged to open up with me seeing that there could be a tangible benefit.

2. They have very short attention spans.

One huge cost of our increasing use of technology is the continuing shrinking of attention spans. In a talk at Google, Imagineering legend Bob Gurr, designer of the Disneyland Monorail, among many other things, was asked how he sees attractions changing in the future. He noted that over the last 50 years he has seen a tremendous change in attention spans.

Gurr brilliantly defines attention span as the time it takes for someone to get bored and he notes that for some today it is as short as 20 seconds.

> 50 years ago people would do any kind of an activity and it would be kind of simple, kind of slow. They would spend quite a few minutes at something. The attention span of some people, I think, is right around 20 seconds. You can be bored in about 20 seconds if something is not really interesting. The interesting thing about that is the stuff that we spend such a short time at are usually mind-blowing technical achievements. And that goes back to this curve I was trying to describe. It's like how much more do we have to do in the face of people who, maybe in 10 years, they'll be down to 15 seconds before they are bored? That really impacts storytelling because you can't get people to sit down and savor a story — savor all the subtleties of something... What do you do to get their attention so that they'll savor the whole idea?

This does not mean our kids can't pay attention. I'll discuss this in depth in later chapters, but my students rarely have difficulty staying focused in my class. I can often hold their attention during a lecture for the full 45 minutes. Yes, seriously. We just have to recognize that our lectures need to modernize and adapt. We have plenty of engaging presentation tools available to help combat boredom. Attention and entertainment matter. We want kids to "savor our whole idea" so what do we do to get, and hold, their attention? We can start by using the ideas of those whose very job is to do so, the Disney Imagineers. Disney stays in business by keeping their guests engaged. We have a slight advantage in that our kids are, sadly, conditioned to think school is boring before they even meet us. We don't have to do much differently to have our classes stand out and rise above their expectations. A little Disney magic in the classroom can go a long way toward staving off boredom and holding their attention.

3. They have a ton on their plate.

As a teacher, especially at the secondary level, it is very hard to remember how much our kids are expected to do and learn in a single day. I often get frustrated when they seem to not remember the things I had just taught them the day before (or sometimes just 10 minutes ago!) We have to step back and remember that 4 to 5 other teachers also taught them stuff the day before. Plus, of course there was whatever drama that happened at lunch, that argument she got in with mom this morning in the car, the baby sister she has to help take care of when she gets home, the never ending stream of information coming through on social media, and of course softball practice at 6.

This will come more with later commandments, but knowing that our audience is often overloaded is very important. We need to make sure we present our content in the most concise and engaging manner possible if we're going to break through the din and reach a level where they are truly learning.

4. They are better than we often think they are.
It can sometimes be very difficult to see the good in our students (especially if you teach middle school!) The current generation of students, in many ways, seem less connected to one another than any before. Their relationships are often transient and surface level at best and often nothing more than virtual. This, of course, was only made worse by the forced distanced learning many of them suffered through as a result of COVID quarantines. Many seem undisciplined and disinterested in schoolwork. I've seen plenty of teachers who just give in and say, "This is just what their generation is." They let their students hide in their own world with earbuds in their ears and screens in their eyes, far removed from the collaborative learning we know works best. The philosophy seems to be, "If that's who they are, why fight it? At least it keeps them quiet, right?"

That mentality is equal parts sad and wrong. Our kids can do amazing things when we empower them to do so. Each year I help organize our district holiday food and toy drive. As with any such drive students around the district donate food, toys and clothes. It is wonderful to see our students really get into the giving spirit. However, what amazes me most is the work of the kids who volunteer to help organize the drive. We have a 24-hour window (which, minus sleep works out to about

14 hours of real-time work) to do the whole thing. The event consists of 25 or so adult volunteers and roughly 200 student volunteers. We start on a Friday at 4 PM. We have 4 hours that night to set up everything for the 150 families that will be arriving Saturday morning. Our students start by sorting through the thousands of food items and packing the food into grocery bags. Next, they sort and arrange the clothing onto tables by type, size and gender. While this is happening, about 20 students are working in another room to stuff around 400 stockings and another group is setting up a toy shop in their own corner of the gym. The kids get so excited while they are volunteering. I regularly hear them saying how much fun they are having and how they feel good knowing they are helping others. They do anything and everything we ask of them. Interestingly, many of our volunteers are from the very families we serve the next day!

That next day we, along with many of the same student volunteers, start early in the morning. For 5 or so hours our students serve as ambassadors as they lead the families through the event. They pull wagons for them that they fill with bags of food, clothing and toys. They help the families load their donations into their cars, and they do it with a smile and genuine kindness that I just don't often get to see in the classroom. Our kids want to do good; I just don't think we give them enough opportunities to do so.

Most teenage guests at Disneyland provide further examples of why this negative stereotype is wrong. Let me preface this by telling you how much I hate when people, particularly students, have earbuds in. To me, earbuds communicate very clearly "Whoever I'm with is not important. Only I am. I am going to entertain myself. You don't matter." When I see teachers allowing, some even encouraging, kids to wear them it really bothers me. I've been told, "that's just normal, they always do it." I disagree. When I'm at Disneyland I very, very rarely see earbuds in anyone, even teenagers. What I see instead are families dressed in coordinated t-shirts, groups of teens talking and laughing together, and people striking up conversations with others they've never met. Disneyland doesn't have a rule against earbuds, they don't have to. Instead, they created an environment that allows the friendliness in everyone, including teens, to shine.

We need to recognize that our kids are capable of amazing things and hold them to those very high standards. Expect greatness and you'll see a whole lot more of it!

How to Know Your Audience

When I started teaching I knew almost nothing about my audience. There's a reason people cringe when I tell them I teach middle school. For most it is a scary age to deal with. For me, it was my absolute last choice for teaching. For my student teaching I hoped to teach at the high school level. My degree is in economics and I had worked as a high school tutor during college. I was even willing to do primary grades as I'd volunteered in a second-grade class and loved it. Just please don't make me do middle school! Of course, God knows best and I was placed in a middle school. Further, to top it off, it was the one middle school in my district that I knew nothing about. I was horrified. I absolutely hated middle school as a student. What could I do as a teacher?! It only took a few days for me to realize how wrong I was. Middle schoolers are just big kids. Yes, they are unique, different, moody, and so much more, but they are also joyful, imaginative and loving. (No, really!) I've had offers to "move up" to the high school over the years, but I know, and love, my audience and don't think I'd ever leave.

The adolescent brain is an amazing thing. The way it works, and doesn't, is absolutely fascinating. If you really want to know your audience you will need to read up on the brain. Psychology and neuroscience articles can go a long way in helping to explain why our students sometimes do things that we cannot comprehend. ("I literally just told you what to do and now you're asking about it again?!") With just a little bit of study you will often know your students better than they know themselves.

Admittedly, reading about neuroscience may be a bit boring. Luckily, Disney has us covered. Disney/Pixar's *Inside Out* is a must watch for anyone who works or lives with adolescents. Riley, the 11-year-old girl at the center of the movie, is one of the most realistic portrayals of adolescents in film. The film's writers needed to simplify the brain and emotions, ultimately having just 5 emotions in Riley's head despite having 26 at one point in development. Still, there is incredible depth in what the movie is able to represent. The film is the story of Riley growing up and dealing with how her brain is changing. It represents her childhood as innocent. Her emotions are simple and Joy is usually the one in control. As Riley experiences the challenges of adolescence (in particular a dramatic change in her home life) we see the other emotions take center stage. Anger, Fear and Disgust overwhelm her leading her to make decisions that she would have never made just a couple years ago. Of course, like most adolescents, Riley does not communicate her struggles, but turns further and further inward until she reaches her breaking point. She finally cracks and the healing begins. In the end we see her growing in complexity. Her brain now often mixes emotions with one another. She is starting to see the depth in herself and the world around her.

Riley *is* our audience!

I mentioned before how that simple question of "How are things at home?" can open the floodgates. Like Riley, many kids in our audience today are being asked to cope with things that are way beyond their ability to handle on their own. Many of my students are responsible for multiple younger siblings when they get home after school (and now, even *during* school thanks to quarantines and lockdowns.) Many have to prepare meals, help with homework and get their siblings bathed. They are at an age where their parents assume they are old enough to handle such things. As a result, the expectations of them in terms of responsibility and learning also increase dramatically.

There are other ways to get to know our audience as well. First, we can consider how we feel when in the role of students. The creation of Disneyland, for example, came from Walt's very personal experience with his target audience: he and his two daughters. As noted on the plaque at the entrance of the Main Street Opera House, Walt first conceived the idea of Disneyland while at Griffith Park watching his daughters ride the carousel. He saw them and the other children having a great time while the adults sat around watching passively. This gave him the idea of creating a park that families could enjoy together — a park that provided joyful experiences for all ages. Walt had his audience and he knew it well because he and his daughters *were* the audience! You may no longer be a student, but you certainly were at some point. In some ways, at least, we can know our audience because we are our audience.

Think about any time you've attended a professional development workshop. You'll likely realize why so many people say teachers make the worst students. Why are we, the audience, so disconnected from these experiences? The presentations are often dry and flooded with bad PowerPoint presentations. We see the same 9-minute YouTube videos we saw at the last two workshops. We do the same awful icebreakers. We then are told a bunch of ways to teach material in an engaging way by a person utilizing literally zero of the strategies they are teaching us. We know what it is like to be a student being talked down to. Reflecting on our personal experiences both from when we were in school and from training we receive today helps us know our audience.

Another method is using surveys. Disney relentlessly surveys their guests on their desires and experiences. They even have a name for it — guestology. In the parks one will often come across cast members with a bulky looking tablet and a stylus who will ask you to stop and answer a couple questions. (Please help them out and take the survey, they have a stressfully high hourly quota to fulfill!) They survey at different times and different days. They want a very broad, and frequent, measure of what their audience is thinking.

They take these surveys so seriously that they even guide decisions on what attractions to build next. Soarin' Over California, for example, was designed to meet an unmet desire as shown by guest surveys. According to Mark Sumner, the head technical engineer on the project, Guests were asked "What experience would you like to have at a Disney park that is not currently available?" One answer that kept coming up was flight. The desire to fill that audience request drove the Imagineers to create the incredible attraction.

I've done end of course surveys for a while, but I keep making them more in-depth and I've started adding more throughout the year. Short reflections at the end of an activity not only help students process their learning, but helps me, the designer, find the areas where I can improve the experience. These surveys have revealed some things I would have never predicted. Most notably, every year, a significant chunk of my students choose "taking notes" as their favorite class activity. That means one of two things. Either the other assignments in my class are awful or, somehow, taking notes in my class is particularly enjoyable. I'm pretty sure it's the latter. I work very hard to make my presentations enjoyable, as you will see, but I would not have guessed my students enjoyed them so much if I hadn't seen it in their surveys.

I've also learned about my book audience through surveys! One thing that jumped out was a request for chapter summaries. I also know my audience, just like me, has one thing they can't forget, even if they try — those wonderful Disney songs! So, each chapter will end with a "Makin' Memories" summary page (a reference to a very old Disney song that owners of the *Disney Sing-along Songs* VHS tape from the early 90s will know well!) I've broken the main points of the chapter down to three Disney song titles to help you remember them. Each summary closes with a quote of inspiration from a Disney personality and an idea you can implement in your classroom tomorrow. The book has lots of big ideas, but I wanted to leave you with something you can do right now if you so choose. Doing my best to know my audience!

Makin' Memories

Commandment 1: Know Your Audience

Our audience, our students, changes from year to year. For our educational program to be truly successful we need to know where our students are coming from and where they are going. That information should guide our lesson design and classroom policies.

* * *

Love Is an Open Door

Knowing your audience opens the door for you to create magical experiences for your students. Be on alert for opportunities that fit your students then take a shot. People don't like to say no, especially to teachers.

> *Who can you ask to speak to or provide a surprising experience for your students?*

Poor Unfortunate Souls

Students today are capable of just as much good as any generation before them. They do, however, face unique challenges that we need to understand. They frequently have more responsibilities than we did growing up. Empathy goes a long way to getting to know them.

> *How can you build time into your classroom routine to get to know your students?*

Strangers Like Me

As easy as it is to forget, our students are humans just like us. They have good and bad days. Sometimes their outside world impacts their attitude. We don't have to take it personally. The more you get to know them the easier it is to forgive them.

How does a bad day affect your behavior toward others?

* * *

One Little Spark

"Marty made Imagineers. He had a way of intuiting that people had something more to give, and of finding opportunities for them to do that. This was something much more subtle than just recognition of talent. It was a human thing, a recognition of something inside a person that could be cultivated into the total combination of features it takes to be an Imagineer. That takes a lot of empathy, a lot of attention, a lot of patience and a lot of faith."

—Joe Rohde, Imagineer

There's a Great Big Beautiful Tomorrow

Greet your students at the door. Commit to ask at least 5 of them about their weekend focusing on what they did for fun.

CHAPTER TWO

"Wear Your Guests' Shoes"

Insist that your team members experience your creation just the way the guests do it.

- Marty Sklar, *Dream It! Do It!*

Despite always looking to the future, Walt Disney must have looked back to his daughters riding the carousel in Griffith Park as he looked out over the crowd gathered on Disneyland's opening day. "To all who come to this happy place, welcome. Disneyland is your land." he said. His park had grown from that wild dream formed on that bench to this day with 28,000 guests (twice as many as were given tickets) ready for the experience of a lifetime. "Here age relives fond memories of the past, and here youth may savor the challenge and promise of the future." he continued. "Disneyland is dedicated to the ideals, the dreams and the hard facts that have created America, with the hope that it will be a source of joy and inspiration to all the world."

Only days earlier, Walt was faced with a decision that had no good options. A plumber's strike put construction of the park behind schedule. It became clear that not everything would be done by opening day. The plumbers could finish the restrooms or the drinking fountains, but not both.

Walt put himself in the shoes of his guests. He realized that they could survive without drinking fountains, but not with restrooms. The restrooms were finished just in time. On that unusually hot July day the guests didn't appear very understanding. Some speculated that Walt purposefully built the park without drinking fountains so guests would be forced to buy Coke, a major sponsor. One can only imagine how they would have felt if there were no restrooms!

Though Walt dreamed up Disneyland as a place where he and his daughters could have fun together, he had the joy of his guests in mind from the beginning. "We made this place just for you, our guests." he said. If Disneyland truly was to be their land Walt and the Imagineers would have to know them deeply. In a sense the Imagineers' jobs were done. The park was ready. It was up to the guests now to determine how it would be received and understood., but Walt wasn't finished. He knew Disneyland would continue to grow and change to meet the needs of his guests. The only real way that could happen was for Walt to see and experience the park through his guest's eyes. He had to walk in their shoes.

By opening day Walt had been putting himself in the shoes of his guests for a while. In the months before the park opened Walt was already there walking the site daily, ensuring every detail was just right for his guests. "In those early days you just couldn't escape Walt," said Bill Evans, one of Disneyland's landscape architects, "He toured the place daily." This led him to anticipate problems before the guests even encountered them. In one case he saw a plan for the sidewalks of Main Street, U.S.A. with square corners and said "People aren't soldiers! They don't turn in sharp angles! Curve the sidewalks! Make the corners round!" The designers, whose job it is to make these plans didn't see the potential problem, only Walt with his eyes on his guests did.

After the park opened, Walt Disney continued to learn about his audience by spending time in his park watching his guests — wearing their shoes. Walt was in Disneyland so frequently that he had his own apartment built inside the park. It was built above the Main Street Fire Station, giving him the opportunity to watch his guests any time he wished. The apartment is very small, measuring just over 500 square feet. It is nice, but certainly not lavish. It is still there today, and a lantern is lit in the window signaling Walt's continuing spirit watching over the park.

There are countless stories of Walt walking through the park, talking to guests and cast members to learn what they wanted. My favorite of these stories came early in the construction of the park. Walt was walking down Main Street,

U.S.A. As he walked by the huge store display windows he got down on his knees and looked up. Walt was placing himself in the shoes of his smallest guests, the children. He required the builders to remake the windows, putting them down at eye level for kids, not for adults. He wanted to make sure the kids felt welcome throughout the park, even in the shops they'd surely hate to be stuck in! As Doug Lipp, creator of many of the training lessons at Disney University, writes in *Disney U*, "A common sight was Walt squatting down and then looking up at a building from a lower angle. Walt's equally common comment 'Can you see little kids looking up at this?' kept his planners and designers on their toes. Walt's determination to view the storefronts and buildings from the vantage point of children ensured that the needs of this large population of guests, an often-overlooked group, were addressed."

* * *

Marty Sklar, in *One Little Spark*, points out the importance of anticipating the first impressions of your audience. "Understanding how your customers or guests will first experience your product is fundamental to making it something they will be drawn to and want to experience over and over again." Put yourself in the shoes of your students during their first week of school at the secondary level. They've just met between 5 and 7 new teachers. Each teacher presented a series of rules and gave them a daunting list of expectations and procedures to take home to be signed. What if your first day at a job consisted of you being hammered by 7 different bosses all repeatedly telling you what *not* to do? As the great philosopher Peter Gibbons said in *Office Space*, "I have 8 different bosses right now. So that means that when I make a mistake, I have 8 different people coming by to tell me about it. That's my only real motivation — not to be hassled." That is not the feeling we want our kids leaving our classroom with at any point and especially not on the first day.

This first experience our students have in our classroom is vitally important and we often waste it. We often fill the first day with rules, procedures and tons of papers to be signed. I know that is what we've always done. I know it is often what we feel we're *supposed* to do. Unfortunately, by doing so, we've just sucked the life out of our guests. Would they want to repeat that experience? Would you?

Imagine you are taking your first trip to Disneyland. You've excitedly anticipated your trip for two months, longer really. You've heard stories about how wonderful it is for as long as you can remember. You show up and find the ticket line longer than you'd hoped. That's okay, just a small chink in the armor. You get into the park, see the flowers arranged in the shape of Mickey's head, welcoming you like the studio logo before a movie, and the excitement builds. You head to the left to enter the tunnel. Like watching a fading transition between scenes, you slowly start to see the hustle and bustle of Main Street, U.S.A. on the other side. You are beaming with joy. You stand up straight, proud, and ready to start your adventure.

Then a hand reaches out to stop you. "I'm sorry folks, you can't go in yet. You haven't heard all the rules." The cast member hands you a 3 page, single-spaced typed document that reads "Mr. Disney's Park Rules." The rules open by saying "Welcome to Disneyland! You're going to love it here. These rules and guidelines exist to ensure your experience is a magical one. Please read them all carefully. There may be a quiz!"

The magic is fading quickly, but you begin to read. You make it through three pages of regulations telling you how to treat other guests and when you may get a drink and use the restroom. You have to ask a cast member first of course. You reach the end and sign the document. The cast member who stopped you then gives you a big smile and says, "Now let's talk about the paper you just signed." She proceeds to go over *every* rule you just read in excruciating detail. Is there any magic left?

This sounds ridiculous, of course, but if we push the analogy further things get much worse. Imagine that after signing the document and hearing the discussion you continued on to Tomorrowland. You are ready for Space Mountain! When you reach the entrance, you are stopped by another cast member. She gives you another form to sign with essentially the same rules as the first one. This happens 4 more times throughout your day at Disneyland. Each time the initial joy and excitement drains further.

That is frequently the first day experience for our secondary students. They come in excited (no, really!) filled with hopes and fears. They are ready to take on the world. Then, as the day goes on, they are subjected to syllabus after syllabus. They are told multiple times to "Show respect for one another" and "Read all instructions." The same rules they've heard since kindergarten. Rules so patronizing that at this point they've become offensive. Has any 7th grader ever seen a classroom wall poster with the words "Read all instructions." and then had a life changing epiphany? "OH! It all makes sense now..." It seems unlikely.

Disneyland posts very few rules anywhere in their park. There are some basic ones printed on the park map, almost certainly only for legal reasons, but that's about it. They don't need to point out that it is important to respect other guests or avoid running in the halls. It's pretty obvious and if someone fails to do it, then a cast member can step in and correct that guest.

So, what could a First Day without rules look like in a classroom?

You arrive at your new school wearing your new, nice school clothes. You have your freshly cut hair done perfectly. You walk onto campus, drawn in by the playful music blasting from the speakers. You find your friend from last year and begin to talk excitedly about what is to come. The bell rings and you head to your first class. Getting closer you notice a large poster-sized sign outside the door. You begin to hear the music change from joyful to adventurous. You get close enough to make out the title on the sign, "Magical History Adventure! Starring Mr. Roughton." The music continues to swell as you walk close enough to read the rest; "a thrilling time-travel adventure through history featuring fascinating characters, spectacular events and intense excitement."

Beyond the sign you see your new teacher. He greets you with a huge smile and hands you a card saying, "Welcome aboard!" You make your way to the line and see movie posters on the wall... Well, they look like movie posters, but they have titles like "History Mystery" and "Digging for the Truth." Those aren't movies you've heard of. "Maybe those are part of the adventure," you think to yourself. The music changes again. A narrator begins to speak welcoming you to Time Machine 110. He tells you it is important to keep your hands, arms, feet, and legs inside the vehicle at all times. He explains that the boarding pass you just received has a seat number telling you where to sit inside. He closes with "Enjoy your adventure!" as the classroom door opens and you are welcomed inside.

You find your seat and notice more movie posters around the room. You see a timer counting down on the screen in front of you with a reminder to fill in the information on your boarding pass. The timer ticks down to zero complete with an audio countdown and cheering crowd. A video begins to play on the screen. You've seen that green box before. It looks like a movie trailer. "In a world where teachers can be boring... one man will change your world." Scenes of action and joy play out in front of you. You recognize the carpeting and the toys on the wall. Everything in the video is happening in the room in which you are now sitting. Will you get to do those things this year?!

The video ends and your new teacher finally says something. "Hello everyone, welcome to our school and room 110. I'm Mr. Roughton and you're going to love it here. Today, we're going to learn about the most important thing in the world... me!" You laugh. That sure wasn't what you expected to hear.

For the next 30 minutes Mr. Roughton shares a bunch of objects from his life. There's an old movie ticket, some buttons, a picture of his video game room at home and a click on the shuffle button on his Pandora Radio playlist to see what comes up. You are writing, analyzing, and forming conclusions supported with evidence. He then says, "Okay, time for your first field trip." Wait a minute. You didn't even bring a permission slip! You stand up and walk out the back door to go investigate his car. You have 60 seconds to look through it — you even get to touch it. You realize he never told you not to drive it but, for some reason, you don't try anyway. Neither does anyone else. It's almost like that rule was obvious...

The period ends all too quickly and you are left wanting more. When you get home that night your parents, who have been through plenty of First Days, ask you for all the papers they surely need to sign. They ask where the one from social studies is. You realize then you never got one, but you can't wait to tell them everything that you did in that class that day. Does that sound like a first impression you'd enjoy as a student?

I'll discuss classroom management in greater depth in Chapter 8, but put yourself in the shoes of a student experiencing the First Day I just described. Would you be tempted to misbehave? Would you even have time to do so? When students are engaged most management takes care of itself. When students feel respected, trusted and empowered alongside being engaged nearly all management takes care of itself. Wear their shoes and have some fun!

Having a First Day like this makes your students excited to see what is to come. Marty Sklar used the example of the Dumbo attraction at Walt Disney World to illustrate the importance of properly setting up an experience. The attraction is one of the most popular for kids at the Magic Kingdom in Florida. As a result, the wait times were getting very long. While no one likes waiting in line, nobody hates it more than kids. Something had to be done. Ultimately the line was moved into an indoor big top filled with playground equipment. Kids could now play while waiting. This is what it means to wear your guests' shoes. Adults don't need a slide to help pass the time in line, but kids sure do.

We can use similar strategies to make our day to day activities much more engaging for our students. One activity that I do often is close reading of historical texts. I try to find the most interesting readings I can, but a sheet of text often looks like a line in the hot Florida sun waiting to ride Dumbo to my 7th graders. So, I built a playground around it! I named the activity HA!, short for Historical Analysis. I put a picture of Nelson from *The Simpsons* and his trademark "Ha ha!" in the corner. I added a section for interacting by drawing pictures and another for students to represent their feelings on the text with emojis. None of that changed what the lesson was or the skills required to complete it. It is simply anticipating where my guests will lose interest or become frustrated and trying to prevent it as much as possible.

How to Wear Your Guests' Shoes

Of course, all this begs the question, how do we do it? How do we wear our students' shoes?

One method I discovered from one of my master's degree courses is called a narrative observation. In it you choose one student as your observation focus. For an entire lesson you write the student's performance and experiences as a narrative story. By looking at your observation as a story you end up focusing on more, and different, details than you would have otherwise. In a story, characters have feelings and setting matters. With this observational style you are recording their feelings through descriptions of facial expressions, body language and word choice. "When Jenny read question 4 her face clearly showed confusion and doubt." This provides a much deeper view of the lesson than if you simply stood back and observed the class at large performing it.

The first time I did this was for one of my History Mystery labs. In these activities students analyze artifacts and testimony from history to try to solve a mystery. This particular one tasked students with finding out who was behind the assassination of Giuliano de Medici. It was my first History Mystery and had been revised multiple times over five years before doing the observation. It has always been one of my most popular lessons both with students and with other teachers. I didn't expect to learn much. I honestly chose it because I felt it was the easiest one I could do to complete the assignment! My students move freely throughout the activity without much additional guidance from me so I could easily pick a student to observe with no one knowing anything was different. The student I chose was an English Learner with a good grade in the class. As she traveled with her group she worked diligently, as she always did. What I did not expect was how much she struggled with certain questions on the sheet. The answers to the questions really aren't important to the lesson. They are just there to guide the investigation, but the word usage on some really threw her off. I've never worn the shoes of a 12-year-old, female, English Learner so while I had adjusted the reading level for 7th graders there was still work to be done to remove the barriers to her learning. It was a powerful experience that I've since repeated and highly recommend.

Another way to wear your student's shoes is to observe other classrooms. Of course, there is a ton we can learn from watching our colleagues, but this is more about watching the students in those classrooms. We often form assumptions of our students based on what we experience with them in our class. However, we all know that kids react and respond differently in different situations. Sometimes all it takes is one change in the environment to change them completely. That change could be another student, different expectations or a simple procedure. By observing another environment, we can learn how we might improve our own.

Now, let's get really Disney. Walt didn't just observe his guests from his apartment on high. He shared their experiences. There's a story about how he once rode the Jungle Cruise unannounced. He was seemingly just enjoying the experience with the guests. However, after the ride, he fumed at the attraction manager, "What is the trip time for this attraction?" The manager knew Walt's ride time was shorter than it should have been. Walt continued, "How would you feel if you paid to go to the movies and they cut the center reel out of the picture!?" He didn't just witness the guests being short-changed, he experienced it.

We should experience our classroom in the same way. A few years ago, near the end of the school year, my students were doing a group activity. In one of my honors classes one of the groups was short a member who was absent for the day. Being honors kids, one of them argued how this was unfair, though she did it with a smile and was clearly just having fun. A second member piped in and said, "You should be our partner Mr. Roughton." I jumped into teacher mode and quickly reacted explaining why that wouldn't be fair to the rest of the groups.

About a minute later I realized this was a great opportunity to get down in the trenches with my kids. I sat down in the empty desk and said, "All right, let's do this!" They were stunned. They didn't expect me to *actually* join them. It turned out to be a world-changing experience for them and for me.

I've always been very interactive with my students. I walk around chatting and joking with them as they work. This made me realize, however, that I always do it *over* them. Sometimes I'll kneel down to get on their level, but there is something magical about sitting in a chair at a desk next to them and working alongside them.

The lesson happened to be the perfect one for this experiment. The groups read 6 information dossiers about famous pirates and had to argue which was the most villainous. It didn't require much from me as the teacher so the groups could pretty easily run themselves. That allowed me to fully take on the role of a student. I made sure not to be the teacher. The group had a lot of fun with it. They started calling me Arianna (the absent student). I ran with it. I (lovingly) mocked Arianna's trademark hair twirl and gum smack. I provided answers like a group member would and made sure to ask questions like one as well.

I learned a lot about how they worked as a team and navigated through the lesson. I also found that the lesson had a bit too much content to fit into the time I had allotted. We managed to get through the dossiers, but we didn't leave much time in our group for discussion and debate. The group took their papers home and finished the final question alone. The other groups had a similar issue. This wasn't a new thing. I've done the lesson before and it has always been this way. The difference this time is that I personally felt the failure. I wanted to discuss what we'd read with the group and I couldn't because of the time pressure. I didn't realize how important it was to provide time for that until I myself experienced missing it. This led me to simplify and shorten some of the readings so that the next time it came around the students would have enough time for the discussion as a group. I wore their shoes and learned things I would not have otherwise, and I also had a great time!

I built more of a relationship with those kids in 25 minutes than I had in the rest of the year. It was such an awesome experience that I turned it into a power up reward for my class game, Fracture Crisis, which I'll explain later. Students reaching level 9 may force me to be their partner for any collaborative activity. They think they are putting one over on me (and of course I play it up big time that they are), but really they are providing me with a joyous and extremely useful experience.

This experience taught me the importance of doing my new lessons before using them with students. If for some reason you can't wear their shoes yourself, have someone else do it! I've become pretty adept at predicting how long students will take on a given activity, but whenever I'm doing something different from my normal routine, I've learned to have someone else go through it first. This is especially important with complex, multi-step activities like a Breakout. Breakouts are lessons modeled around the Escape Room concept. They consist of a series of puzzles that are cracked, often in sequence. They are designed specifically to operate under a time limit. Whenever I've tried using one designed by another person, I've found the clues to be far too vague and the overall experience somewhat frustrating. As a result, I've designed my own to better fit my students and content.

Predicting how long a 12-year-old will take to solve a puzzle is very difficult. Since I made the puzzle and know the solution there's really no way to test it myself. I can time how long it takes to complete the readings and they take a guess on the time to reach the solutions, but that seems incomplete at best. It is helpful to have a group of students try your lessons before everyone else. My first class of the day gets the honor of being my beta testers for many of my activities. I used to just call them "guinea pigs,", but eventually realized that telling students "I'm going to experiment on you as an unimportant object before I try it on important people" was not the message I wanted to be sending. Recently, I created a new activity called Time Warp which is modeled after point-and-click adventure games like those made by Telltale Games. Students take on the role of a historical character and make decisions to try to advance through the game successfully. I wanted it to feel as much like a game as possible, so I used the beta testers term with the class as a last minute idea and they completely ran with it. Firstly, they knew what a beta tester was. I don't know if any student has understood the guinea pig metaphor without me explaining it. One excitedly asked, "What do we do if we find bugs?!" Great question! I have no idea! I quickly threw together a semi-official looking bug report form and gave them password protected access. They really felt like they were part of something special and I got much more detailed information about the activity from them than I would have otherwise.

And of course, I should have known this. I've been a beta tester for various games and software programs. I know all I'm doing is unpaid testing work for the company. Still, there's something magical about being on the inside — being the one in the know. Just having the title of beta tester gives me a connection to the product far deeper than I'd usually have. I feel like I'm part of it. That's partly why Disney can charge tens of thousands of dollars for access to their private restaurants like 21 Royal and Club 33. The experience is incredible, but the lifelong bragging rights of saying you ate in one of them is arguably even better. (Take that from someone who has eaten in Club 33!) So, at least sometimes, wearing our guest's shoes can be as simple as putting ourselves in the proper mindset. Would I want to be a guinea pig? Nope. I'd sure like to be a beta tester though!

A quick side note on the words we use with our students. Disney is very deliberate about word choice throughout their company knowing it has a great impact on people's feelings and opinions. The very wording of this commandment is an example. Disney refers to their customers as guests. Some resorts use "visitors" or "patrons" which both sound better than customers, but neither is as welcoming as "guest." Employees are called cast members because they are part of the show. I much prefer being called an educator over a public employee. It's empowering. I learned very early in my career not to call my 7th graders kids! They at least want to be students, but we can call them scholars if we really want to empower them.

As fun as it is to be a beta tester, it can be somewhat unfair to your first period to always have to take on that responsibility. If you don't want to saddle one of your classes with always having to do the untested version of your activity, you can have a colleague try out your lesson. Walt frequently walked the park, but he also insisted that his managers do the same. He wanted them to experience how each attraction, line queue and situation felt for the guests. I've found that having my colleagues experience my lessons can be very effective as well, and vice versa. One of my colleagues for years talked up one of his lessons on the Mayans. He shared the worksheet and PowerPoint file with me and told me all about it. I didn't get it. I mean, I got what to do — I just didn't get *why*. I didn't see how it could be effective. It wasn't until I sat with him and actually did it myself that the light bulb went off. He was right. It is amazing. It became one of my favorite lessons and the basis for many other activities I designed. (I'll discuss this lesson type which we call Digging for the Truth later in Chapter 10.)

We need to get more comfortable watching one another teach. Teaching is such a solitary job that many of us are afraid to let other adults into our space and observe. We're afraid they are going to judge us negatively. In some cases, sadly, those fears may be justified, but there is simply no better way to wear your students' shoes than to visit their classes. We have to push past that fear. I'm grateful to have colleagues who are willing to risk judgment and share their lessons and let me observe their classes. I wish it happened more often!

Seeing how students behave in their different classes can be eye-opening. For example, seeing one of my students actively participate in one of their classes when they were always hesitant to do so in mine led me to make important changes that helped many of my students. Seeing them in another element also lets us see which students they associate with or avoid. I'd love to be able to just shadow a student for an entire day. I don't think we truly appreciate how much they are asked to do in every class. Wearing their shoes for a day would go a long way towards building our own classes with empathy.

Another great option is to simply spend time with your students. Get to know them. Learn what movies, shows and music are in. If you're truly courageous you can even visit your students on their turf at lunch — the dreaded lunchroom. This was actually how I started my journey to get to know my students. For the first few years I taught, I'd head down to the cafeteria and sit and eat with my students. While my own students were pleasant to be around (probably because their teacher was sitting there!) the rampant profanity, disregard of trash and flying carrots from the other students turned this into a chore more than a joy. Still, I learned quite a bit about my audience. I learned, for example, that middle schoolers don't particularly seem to like eating carrots. Secondly, I learned why my 5th period class right after lunch always seems to come in wired and out of control. Lastly, I learned that some of my students would greatly appreciate having a safe place to go during lunch.

As a result, I started opening my room daily at lunch. My room is open for students to come in and get out of the over-whelming crowds in the lunchroom (just like the Dumbo tent getting guests out of the hot Florida sun!) I have a closet full of board games that we play a few times a week. Additionally, we watch anime on Wednesdays and play video games on Friday. Disney music is on the menu almost every day! I use any excuse I can to interact with them on a personal level. So many of our students are aching for attention and that is very hard to do during class. There's just too many kids and not enough time. I treasure this time spent with my students as humans, not just as students. I get to know them, but just as importantly, they get to know me.

I've learned so much about my students individually and corporately from these lunch experiences. Other teachers have asked me with wonder, "How do you know so much about everything going on?" Easy. The students tell me! By wearing their shoes and being one of them during our break it opens up lines of communication that would otherwise be closed. Other teachers have told me they need a break from the kids. Sometimes, so do I. I get it. On those days I still let the students in and I just stay at my desk. They learn pretty quickly if I need time to myself and they just go right on playing the games without me. That said, I do my best to be available to them every day. It is worth it for the information I pick up and the relationships I build.

Let's go back to Walt's dedication quote. "To all who come to this happy place. Welcome. Disneyland is your land." If Walt can create such an incredible space specifically for his guests, then surely we can try to do the same with our classrooms. If we build them for ourselves then it isn't their land. If it is our land, then they are just visitors. That's not the buy-in we want. Walt went on to say, "We have to meet the needs of the people who come here." Unless we get down in the trenches and wear our students' shoes, we are not going to be able to meet those needs. We can't follow them home and live their lives (nor, in many cases, we would want to), but we certainly can do so in our classrooms and in our schools. Once we do, designing and building with their needs in mind becomes much, much easier.

Makin' Memories

Commandment 2: Wear your guest's shoes

To truly understand how our instructional program affects our students we need to live it ourselves and do our best to see things from their perspective.

* * *

First Day of School

First impressions are important and hard to change. Think deeply about what experience you want your students to have on their first day and plan with that in mind. The first day doesn't have to be filled with rules and procedures. That can come in time as needed. Wow them!

What will you do your next First Day to wow your audience?

I Wan'na Be Like You

We may need to go out of our normal routine to wear our students' shoes. Try observing other teachers, going to the student lunchroom or being a member of a group in your classroom.

*Which teachers at your school (or not!)
might let you come in and observe?*

Be Our Guest

Make your room an inviting place to be so your students will volunteer information about themselves. You won't even have to seek it out. Invite them into your room during non-class times. Talk with them. Play games with them. Let them know they are always welcome!

*What events can you plan outside of class time
to get students to come to your classroom?*

* * *

One Little Spark

"In the year before Disneyland opened, you just couldn't escape Walt. He toured the place daily."

—Bill Evans, Disney Legend

There's a Great Big Beautiful Tomorrow

Take a deep breath then walk to the student lunchroom. Buy your lunch there. Sit and just take in the atmosphere or, even better, sit with some of your students for a chat. Smile!

CHAPTER THREE

Organize the Flow of People and Ideas

Make sure there is a logic and sequence in your stories and in the way guests experience them.

—Marty Sklar, *Dream It! Do It!*

As the clock turned to 11:58 PM my annoyance turned to frustration. It was late. It was cold. My students were all accounted for. They made it back to the meeting spot under the water tower by their 11:55 PM deadline. They knew the consequences if they didn't — 100 words per minute late. When I released them into the wilds of Knott's Berry Farm 5 hours earlier, I reminded them there would be parents waiting at our school at this very late hour to pick up their kids. I would not be happy if their selfish choices led to those parents having to wait a minute longer. It was a simple issue of respect. Don't be late.

How then could I explain that one of our teachers was among those who were not yet back?

A minute later the teacher hurriedly walked up with a few of his students. Breathlessly he said, "I'm sorry. There was a train and we got lost. I swear, I've been to this park dozens of times and I still can't find my way around!" In my self-righteousness I didn't want to hear it. *I* made it back on time, why couldn't everyone?

With a little reflection, I realized he had a point. Knott's does have a fairly confusing layout.

Upon entering, there are three different pathways one can take and they all lead to very different places. Each path curves in such a way that you really can't tell where they are leading. You can generally assume that the path left will take you to the

Ghost Rider roller coaster since you can see it towering in that direction. The path right, thankfully, has a statue of Snoopy in a canoe so that's likely the direction to Camp Snoopy. The path forward? No clue whatsoever as to where it could lead. Each path winds, seemingly aimlessly, around the park. From the back of the park it is the same layout with multiple pathways, but with even fewer landmarks to guide you. Plus, as my colleague noted, there is a train that runs through the middle of the park closing off two different pathways to the entrance at regular intervals.

I guess instead of being frustrated that one colleague didn't make it back, I should have been elated that 30 of my students did!

* * *

Walt and his Imagineers designed Disneyland using a unique hub and spoke pattern in order to facilitate the flow of guests. Upon entering the park your only real option is to go forward. There is a small illusion of choice in that you can go forward via one of two tunnels, one on your right and one on your left, which allow you to pass under the train tracks so they don't cause any disruption of flow. Both lead you in the same direction. You enter onto Main Street, U.S.A. The path still only leads in one direction and you are drawn that way by the splendor of Sleeping Beauty's castle at the end.

Reaching the end of that first straight path is only the beginning. When you arrive at the central plaza in front of the castle you see the true genius of the park's layout. From that point, where the iconic "Partners" statue of Walt holding Mickey's hand now stands, you can see the entrances to each of the park's 4 original lands. Clear pathways lead in each direction. Further, each land has its own clearly visible landmark, known as a wienie, to help guide you along the way. You are left with no doubt about what is coming next. This helps keep guests flowing as they don't have to stand around figuring out their next move.

In our classrooms we should ensure we keep things flowing as well. Having clear and repeated routines is a great starting point. Students should know what they are supposed to be doing in your classroom before they walk in the door. They shouldn't have to ask (even though many still will.) In my room the routine is simple. Students sit down and immediately get to work copying the agenda for the day into their planner. The agenda is on the left side of the board in the same spot every day. They then follow whatever instructions are written on the board. Sometimes the instructions are as simple as "Take out your Chromebook and log in. Then go to this page." I'll then have a big arrow drawn pointing to the screen with the link highlighted. Everything flows from left to right and I use arrows any time there are new directions. Starting class this way every day, starting literally with day one where I explain the layout and routine to my new students outside before they come in, ensures that they know where they are going every day.

In addition to our routines, our seating arrangement can also help facilitate flow in our classrooms. My classroom is set up in a very traditional 6 by 6 grid with one small adjustment, the middle lanes of the grid are a bit wider than all the rest.

This set-up works well for many reasons. First, it gives my students some space for breathing room. There is a trend in education known as flexible seating where students choose where to sit on a daily basis and desks are replaced by bean bags, yoga balls and many non-traditional types of furniture. Along with this they can choose who to sit with. At least at the middle school level, I'm not a fan. The idea is to encourage comfort and collaboration, but honestly, most of what I've seen of it makes me feel like wandering through Knott's Berry farm. I love the idea of comfort. I don't like the idea of disorganization. Many of my students are well below grade level in reading and giving them space to focus is very important. Beyond that, many of my more introverted students are literally exhausted by the interactions forced by constant grouping. Some of my favorite places at Disneyland are those quiet little corners where I can get away from the crowd for a few minutes. Whether it's the lobby of Turtle Talk with Crush or the back alleys of New Orleans Square (before they closed them off for 21 Royal!) it is just nice to have a moment of relative peace. My students have plenty of time to collaborate, my set-up just ensures that they have a break from it.

Secondly, when I do want my students to work collabora-tively, this layout allows me to quickly and easily group my desks. I can have my students in groups of 2, 4 or 6 in about 30 seconds. The first time we do an activity with groups of those sizes I show them how to turn the desks to make the groups. It requires very little movement and leaves no question as to who their group members are for the activity. As a student (and still as an adult) finding group members was always a source of anxiety. Having a structured set-up like this takes that anxiety away. Whenever I set up a new seating chart I tell students to let me know if they cannot work with the people in their 2, 4, or 6 groups they see around them and I may make adjustments. They rarely do. Most kids are happy to work together and are more than happy to be rid of the stress of having to find their own group.

Lastly, this layout allows me fairly easy access to any student. The secret, courtesy of my mentor teacher during student teaching so many years ago Scott Hill, are the wide middle rows. Squeezing myself down the classroom rows with backpacks, jackets and folders on the floor is nearly impossible. The wide middle lanes mean I can easily walk back and forth (and even turn around!) without disruption. I'm not knocking papers or Chromebooks off student desks (usually...) and it limits disruption. The ability to get to my students quickly and easily means I can respond to their questions promptly and I don't have to draw the whole room's attention when I do so. The ability to move freely is a small thing, but an important one.

In early 2019 Disneyland began removing some of the benches around the park. Some people, notably me, were very upset. I simply cannot overstate how much I enjoy sitting. People, notably me, speculated this was done because people sitting aren't people spending. That, however, was not the case. The benches were removed, and in some cases simply moved, as a part of Project Stardust, a multi-year reorganization project designed to facilitate the flow of guests throughout the park. This was done in anticipation of huge crowds expected in the Summer of 2019 due to the opening of Star Wars: Galaxy's Edge. Disney anticipated the flow problem and widened pathways, removed benches, and even moved the location of certain trash cans. When you visit the park today you likely won't even notice the missing benches, but everything does flow just a bit more smoothly.

In the case of Galaxy's Edge, its opening was organized so smoothly that much of the media coverage around the opening of the land in 2019 focused on how empty the park seemed to be. Organizing visits to the new land for the first month was intense. Guests had to get a reservation online or stay in a Disneyland hotel to get in. Many of us have experienced the frustration of hammering the Refresh button on a web browser while trying to buy concert or sports tickets. Disney instead had you open a webpage once and that was it. You just had to leave the page open and it would reload itself when it was ready. My wait was over two full hours, but it was far less frustrating than the typical 15-20 minutes spent refreshing for concert tickets. That was some welcome organization of flow!

On the day you visited the park for your reservation you started in Tomorrowland where you checked in and received a wristband with your time window for visiting Galaxy's Edge. You then made your way to the entrance of the land, of which there are three, but only one was open to keep things organized, where guests lined up before being let in. By the time your group was let in the previous group was on their way out, so it felt like you had the land to yourself. It was an incredible feat of logistics that worked like magic. The fears of overcrowding never came to be, not because attendance was low, but because Disney had organized the flow of people so effectively.

Another great example of Disney organizing movement can be seen any time there is a parade or nighttime spectacular (which is Disneyspeak for a fireworks or projection show) at one of the parks. About 30 minutes before show time white ropes seem to appear magically along the route indicating where guests may sit. Obviously, they are set up by cast members, but it is done with remarkable speed and efficiency. At first guests are free to ignore the ropes, but as showtime closes in, cast members begin directing the crowds to the proper side of the rope lines. Despite blocking off major lines of movement there is surprisingly little disruption to the overall flow of guests in most of the park.

On Main Street, U.S.A. at Disneyland though it gets a little rough. The parade route goes straight down the middle of the street. As a result, thick crowds of guests line the sidewalks on either side. If you are on the Emporium side and absolutely must get your Starbucks fix it would seem you had better do so before the parade starts. Likewise, if you are near the hub and are trying to exit the park, it appears you'd be stuck. The parades can take over 20 minutes and you can't very well just walk through the middle of it, right?

Wrong. You actually can! Each parade has been designed with short breaks throughout. During these breaks cast members quickly open the rope walls at preset points on the route (perhaps not surprisingly, one is right in front of Starbucks.) The parade never technically stops. The music and excitement continue, but that brief opening allows guests to quickly cross the street, right through the middle of the ongoing parade. It's an amazing, and amusing, sight to witness the cast members frantically waving guests across before the next massive float or troop of dancers arrives.

But, what about those guests that are trying to walk down Main Street, U.S.A. to exit the park or up it to enter? The cast members can't very well move the guests sitting to watch the parade. There are pathways through most of the buildings on either side of the street, but those become just as congested as the sidewalks. Too big of an organizational problem? Not for the Imagineers. They have added pathways that go *behind* the buildings on either side of the street. If you want to go up Main Street, U.S.A. towards the castle you can enter the secret path on the Opera House side of the street. If you are going the opposite direction your entrance is hidden behind a small gate on the opposite side between the Jolly Holiday and Coke Refreshment Corner. This path is especially cool as it takes you behind the scenes of the Jungle Cruise! It is likely the only time the average guest will see any "off stage" area of Disneyland. The path on the other side is a covered walkway lined with attraction and movie posters — also cool! Organization at it's very best.

There are many things we can do to make sure the organization of our classroom enhances our classroom experience.

Most of these are simple fixes or tweaks that we can easily make. Make sure your pencil sharpener and box of tissues are easily accessible without disrupting any other students. Have set locations for specific materials that students may need. I have a series of drawers each with their own supplies. They are each clearly labeled "Glue," "Scissors," etc. I have a specific cabinet with art supplies and another with blank white paper. Students know where they are and know they can go get them when needed. I may not be able to make my pencil sharpener exciting, but I can make sure to limit the barriers to accessing it.

The most important flow procedures to have in place in your classroom are those guiding student entry and exit procedures. I'm regularly surprised when I visit other classrooms that don't have clear entry procedures. Students come in socializing and sit down continuing to socialize. The teacher takes roll and then after a couple minutes announces the start of the class. The students take another minute or so to end their socializing and get started.

My room operates much differently. As I stand outside at the door welcoming students the rest come in. They don't wait for a bell to ring. They sit down and begin their daily routine. Do some still socialize? Of course. The majority however take out their planners and copy the daily agenda. They then begin whatever Bellwork task I've left for them on the board. When the bell rings I come in and take roll, often without saying a word. When I'm done and have given them a couple minutes to complete their task I call on students to share. Class is happening already and I haven't had to do anything to lead it. Your routine doesn't have to be so regimented (you need to be yourself as we'll see in chapter 8!), but having a routine of at least some kind sets the tone that your classroom is about learning.

Exit procedures can be equally chaotic. Here, I have to admit, I come up way short. I often teach until just before the final bell leaving little time for clean-up and exit routines. That isn't by design. I try to end my instruction at least three minutes early so we can do those things, but I've yet to figure out how to do so consistently. Admittedly, as a result, the end of my class can be a mess. Ideally, what I'd like to see happen, is my students take a minute to clean up and a couple minutes to complete a short reflection on the day's learning. Doing so helps to ensure that the next period starts off right (since I don't have to scramble to get things in order) and keeps the flow of ideas organized.

Organizing Learning through Story

This goes a long way to organizing the flow of your students, but it does not solve one of the biggest disruptions to flow in the classroom — the dreaded question "I'm done, what do I do now?" My students work and learn at vastly different speeds. I have classes where some students are labeled as gifted while others are reading 5 levels below grade level. Those gifted kids tend to finish quickly. In the past I just had books they could get to read off the shelf. It worked well enough, but didn't really connect with instruction. I tried including more history-themed books, but student interest was low which seemed to defeat the purpose. It also led to having kids constantly getting up wandering the room to get a new book which disrupted some of the flow of other students in the classroom. Now, instead of just the books on the shelf, I have a series of fun enrichment activities called Side Quests which students can find on our class webpage. When students finish early, they don't have to ask, they know where to look to find something to do!

These side quests play directly into my next level of organization, my classroom story. Every classroom tells a story and the most effective ones are built around that story. As Imagineer Doris Hardoon Woodward said, "It all starts with a story!" Humans have organized their ideas around stories for as long as recorded history. At Disneyland each land tells its own story (and only one story as we'll see later) to draw you into the experience. In Adventureland you see overgrown trees and hear thumping drums alongside bird chirps and squawks. In Tomorrowland the plants are neatly aligned and the buildings all have sharp angles, the complete opposite of what you'd find in Fantasyland! What stories are your classroom and curriculum communicating to your students?

I primarily teach 7th grade World History. The state curriculum guide starts with events in 44 B.C. and goes all the way to 1800 A.D. It includes the Roman Empire, China, Japan, West Africa, the Middle East, Latin America, The Renaissance and the Enlightenment. The state also recently added units about Persia, India, and Mongolia. Teaching all that in one year is basically impossible. I can live with that. I've just accepted that some topics won't get taught. What I cannot live with though is the extreme disconnect from one topic to the next. Finding a narrative that ties together such disparate times and locations is an ongoing challenge. It's so bad that at one point in the year I jump from the 1500s in Latin America to the early 200s in China. If I followed the state recommended unit order, it would be even worse. It goes from Rome to Arabia to China to Africa to Japan then back to Europe for the Middle Ages. There's no historical story thread that ties those disparate civilizations together.

To help bring in some unity, one thing I do in each unit is focus on the main people involved. Since we jump from place to place around the world using the general human story is a good connector. I've developed tons of different activities to do this, all with the same goals and expectations, just a slightly different narrative package. Sometimes my kids will make trading cards based around the characters complete with Historical Importance and Interest power ratings. Other times they will be poets creating bio-poems about the person. This a start and it helps bring somewhat of a story, but it still isn't completely unified.

A similar problem exists in other subjects and grade levels. Our science classes jump from cells to rocks. ELA is writing argumentative essays one week and analyzing poetry the next. Elementary classrooms have it even tougher. They jump not just from topic to topic, but subject to subject! Organizing these ideas around an academic narrative is nearly impossible. Teachers have tried for decades and, in our failure to do so, we've been faced with the dreaded question of "why do I have to learn this?" We need a story!

The best way to bring a narrative organization is to make your own story. Gamification is the process of turning an activity into a game, usually by wrapping it in a fictional story, adding leaderboards and some type of player reward system. This has become a popular method of organizing classrooms in recent years. When I first started the process, I focused heavily on the reward aspect. As students earned XP they leveled up and each new level meant new classroom rewards. It was really cool... I thought. The students were initially interested in the rewards, but few engaged in the reward layer as the year went on and they leveled up. I tried many different ways of informing them what rewards were available, but it just felt like it was too much for most kids to keep track of. What I found they really did enjoy was the overall narrative of the game and I found it in a very surprising way.

The story of my class game, *Fracture Crisis,* is that someone in the future is going back in time to change history with the goal of making it so the United States was never created. He or she has been operating undetected for years and has caused an untold number of fractures, or changes, in history. My students have been recruited into an agency known as the Department of Timeline Security, or DTS. Their job is to learn history as it was before the villain came along and started making changes. They then report what they've learned to the Department of Timeline Security with the hopes of rebuilding the Timeline and saving the future.

The first year I ran the game that set up was basically all there was to my story. I made an awesome introduction video complete with Hollywood-style narration and effects. I also re-themed the visuals of some of my presentations to look more futuristic, but made few other changes. I honestly thought the story was just to serve as the entry point to the game and then the rewards would carry the rest. I had rewards like earning a piece of candy, choosing where to sit for a week and having a partner on an otherwise individual activity. To me, that's all gamification meant — giving rewards for levels of achievement. Then the students started asking more and more questions. Who is the DTS? Where are they from? Will we get to fight the villain? All great questions! I made some small narrative additions throughout the year and thought I had done a good job.

The last day of school showed me how wrong I was. After giving my end-of-the-year goodbyes one of my students raised his hand and asked, "So, what about the Fracture Crisis? Did we win or what?" Um. Yes. Sure. You won. High five! Apparently, they cared more about the story than I realized. Looks like I failed to know my audience! It was such a huge letdown for them and I realized how much of an opportunity I had missed out on. I could have organized the entire flow of my classroom from the first day to the last around this story and it would have kept my students, at least many of them, engaged.

So, in year two of the game I simplified the rewards system and built far more of the narrative into the class. I added a second semester restart that explained why they lost all their XP called The Cataclysm. I added new intro narratives to every unit helping to tie those disconnected world history units to each other in a fictional, but effective, way. Why jump from 1500s Latin America to 200s China? Because a new series of Fractures were just detected there by the Department and it might be our best chance to catch our time traveling terrorist!

One great thing about having a narrative game layer to your class is that you have many options for themes to tie your content together. You aren't just limited to specific content-based themes. What about a science course built around medieval fantasy where science plays the role of magic? What about an adventure theme for a math class where every math problem is a puzzle to solve that gets you one step closer to a lost treasure? A western themed English class where the duels play out as debates or poetry slams? Why not? There's so much you can do once you have organized around a theme. We'll look more closely at how to implement those themes in Chapter 7: Tell One Story at a Time.

Another benefit to these narrative structures is students begin to play a role bigger than themselves. It is easy for a student to lose interest in the stories of people half a world away who died over a thousand years ago. I may find the Magna Carta fascinating, but my 12-year-old students generally do not. I've tried linking it to the Constitution and our democracy in general, but they don't particularly care about that either. Many of my students have had little to no social studies instruction in elementary school. So, not only are my topics disconnected, so are my students! By putting them in the role of the hero I give them more motivation to join in. When they hear that the Magna Carta is the document that signifies the birth of the modern world and that removing it from history might remove them too, they have plenty of reasons to get interested. It isn't foolproof and it doesn't work with every student, but it sure works better than "this will be on a test."

Star Wars: Galaxy's Edge is a perfect example of how an overarching story can tie together different, and sometimes, confusing experiences. If you choose to engage with the game layer, which you can completely ignore, the land takes on a life of its own. You choose which side of the galactic battle to support and complete tasks to earn points for your team. You also unlock individual rewards for your character like new clothing options and titles. I became so engaged that I found myself bowing in reverence to a stormtrooper who chastised me and cheering on a rebel who streaked by, with her spear at the ready, clearly on the way to an important mission. I became part of the story.

But, if I step back from the narrative, what was I really doing? I was waiting in line, melting in the hot June sun, waiting in another line, spending a ton of money and then waiting in more lines. None of which would have made for a particularly thrilling event on their own (okay, admittedly spending the money was fun as I got some great stuff!) and don't seem connected in the least. Without the storyline of the game throughout the land it would have just been a series of disconnected experiences. It would have been (gasp!) an amusement park or a carnival, not a Disney experience. The story made it real and made it matter.

Having a narrative layer operating above everything you do helps a ton with organization. However, at Disneyland, it is not only the story of the lands that organize your experiences. Every attraction, restaurant and store are organized around their own story as well. While those stories always fit the theme of their lands, they make each attraction unique. For example, Toy Story Midway Mania sits in the Pixar Pier land of Disney California Adventure. It is, essentially, a modern shooting gallery. It has a series of galleries, each themed after the old games you'd find at a midway — ring toss, dart shooting, etc. Each game also has, not surprisingly, a *Toy Story* theme. That seemed to be the extent of the story to me and, apparently, to most other park guests as well.

As a result, about 10 years after the ride opened Disney Imagineers made one very small change to the attraction to help bring out the story. Today, as you exit the ride, you walk past a room that appears to be a home office. It seems out of place. On the floor of the room is a colorful, open, cardboard package. Looking closely, one sees that it is a package for a game titled "Toy Story Midway Games." It has game descriptions like "5 games of skill!" and "3D Action!" Looking more closely one finds that a smaller box, also empty, with signage showing it is the "Toy Story Tram" that comes with the game. The story of the ride is made clear. You aren't just playing through a modern, highly technical, shooting gallery with random Toy Story characters. You are playing in Andy's imagination. You are one of his toys.

So, this begs the question. If the story wasn't clear before, why does adding this little touch, after the ride is already over, even matter? Why does the story matter? The ride was intensely popular before adding the extra detail often running the second longest waits in the entire park. So, doesn't this just prove that story isn't that important? Obviously not or I wouldn't have used it as my example!

Once one realizes the story the attraction is telling, the next time riding it becomes an entirely new experience. When the attraction starts you sit in your tramcar (looking exactly like the one on the box). You head into the tunnel and see lots of classic toys and games along the walls. They are big, but not overtly so. As you continue to careen and twist down the tunnel the toys and games get bigger and bigger. No, wait. They aren't getting bigger, you're getting smaller! I frequently wondered why that opening 15 seconds of the attraction existed. You don't really do anything, but get jostled around and see a bunch of seemingly random toys. Just get me into the shooting part, that's what the ride is about, right? Wrong. It is about telling the story of you becoming one of Andy's toys and playing out that experience. The story makes it so each part of the attraction is enjoyable.

Likewise, when our lessons tell a complete story we can make every piece important. We, as teachers, know the importance of things like comprehension questions and reading a passage multiple times. Students, not so much. When we provide a story we give them a reason to find those tasks, which aren't very interesting on their own, important and help improve learning outcomes.

One area where my students have long struggled is differentiating among the three major cultures we study in Latin America; the Aztecs, the Maya and the Inca. I decided to design a narrative-based lesson to highlight the differences. I took a fairly standard document-based question activity and added a story. In it students visit a series of locations and examine artifacts found there. Their goal is to figure out which of the three civilizations they are in. But, why?

The narrative begins with a video that opens with the line "It was the opportunity of a lifetime, a chance to travel back in time." Students see a time machine and a view of Earth from space. Then "but something went horribly wrong" pops up on the screen. Things speed up as the time machine crashes toward the Earth. The last image students see is a satellite shot of Latin America. The screen goes black, they hear a crash, and a young woman's voice saying with fear in her voice, "I don't know where I am." Then they "wake up" in an unknown jungle. The only way the Department of Timeline Security can get them out is if they can report back on exactly where they are. Now there is a very good reason to analyze the locations and artifacts. The students have become part of something bigger.

Sometimes we don't even have to make a new story. We already have one and we just fail to use it. I hated my 7th grade history class when I was a student because all we did was label maps, define key terms and answer multiple choice questions. From my perspective there was no rhyme or reason to any of it. There was no story. It was like we just took the shortest path to reach our destination possible, but I had no idea why we were going there in the first place! Here's the content, the test is coming, learn it. That was the flow and it didn't work.

Similarly, my current students struggle when we give them shortcuts without a story. I see this frequently with my kids in their math classes. In 7th grade, when they first learn to solve one step equations using fractions, they are taught the "cross multiplying" shortcut. Earlier that year they learned "cross canceling" when multiplying fractions so there's immediately some confusion. We'll discuss that later in Chapter 7 when we look at the importance of sticking to one story at a time. The real problem with cross multiplying isn't the mix up with cross canceling. It's that many students never get the story behind why they are doing it. They only get the shortcut. If I ask them why they can cross multiply on one problem, but not on another they rarely know. They end up trying to cross multiply any time they see any fraction. They know how to do it; they just don't know why. That's the cost of skipping story! Having a story helps students connect the ideas and skills we teach to other learning and situations.

Another benefit of organizing around a story is that when we have to repeat tasks, we can still make them feel new and unique. Disneyland, for example, shares a very similar attraction to Midway Mania called Buzz Lightyear's Astro Blasters which opened only a few years earlier. It too is a high-tech shooting gallery and it too is based on *Toy Story*. Yet, the two attractions are unique because of their stories and improvements in technology. In Astro Blasters you play as a member of Star Command trying to stop the evil General Zerg. You shoot at physical targets with different shapes to denote their values. Quite different from playing a series of digital 3-D midway games!

In our classrooms we often have to repeat very similar tasks or activities. Things like vocabulary, reading and skills practice are going to happen multiple times in your classroom throughout the year. Without a story this becomes an entry point for the dreaded "When am I ever going to use this in my life?" question. (Notably, I've been to Disneyland dozens if not hundreds of times at this point and I've never once have I asked myself "When am I ever going to use this in life?" while I was there.) Of course, we'd all love it if "You're not, but because I'm a trained professional and I know what is best for your growth and learning just do it." was a sufficient answer. Honestly though, that answer isn't even sufficient for us. I know I ask my doctor plenty of times "Why do I have to do that?" when he recommends I change up my lifestyle or eating habits (and sometimes I just ignore him like when he told me to stop going to Disneyland because my knee is already arthritic.) We need a story, especially on these repetitive tasks.

Our design starts with story and so too does engagement, but it takes something to draw students into that story. A little convincing, a little hook may be all it takes!

Makin' Memories

Commandment 3: Organize the flow of people and ideas

Our classrooms should be organized to best support our learning environment and our lessons should be organized around a story to ensure a clear flow from beginning to end.

* * *

A Whole New World

Arrange your classroom in the way that best fits you and your goals. Consider things like flow of movement, quick grouping for collaboration and placement of things like pencil sharpeners as you build your new world.

*What small layout changes could you make
to improve flow in your classroom?*

We Know the Way

Our lessons make sense to us because we can see the whole thing from beginning to end. Our students aren't always able to see that path clearly. When we wrap our lesson in a story it is easier for them to stay on track throughout the lesson. Try to make sure your lessons have a beginning, middle and end.

*How can you turn a lesson into a story? (Remember,
the story doesn't have to be relevant!)*

Zero to Hero

Organizing your class around a story is a first step toward gamification, running your class like a game. A proper narrative for your class game makes your students into a hero. You can make your sometimes mundane content exciting by making it part of a grand story where your students play the role of hero.

> *What type of theme could you use for your classroom story? Adventure? Western? Comedy?*

＊ ＊ ＊

One Little Spark

"It all starts with a story."

—Doris Hardoon Woodward, Imagineer

There's a Great Big Beautiful Tomorrow

Make some simple rearrangements in your classroom. Try to free up some of the choke points that inhibit movement, label your supply drawers or move the pencil sharpener to a more central location.

CHAPTER FOUR

Create a Wienie

"Create visual 'targets' that will lead visitors clearly and logically through your facility."

-Marty Sklar, *Dream It! Do It!*

The cast member held up a finger and asked the waiting guests, "Any parties of one?" Without a hint of loneliness or shame, I raised my hand. She walked toward me, unclipped the chain like a bouncer removing the velvet ropes to admit a VIP, and waved me forward. I walked proudly past the other guests, who were saddled with things like friends and loved ones, to take my spot on Soarin' Over California.

Being a Single Rider certainly has its benefits.

I continued my VIP walk past the 20 or so guests waiting in both gates A and B, who didn't seem to even notice my clearly special status, to boarding gate C where I took my spot in the back of the pre-show queue line. From here I had a clear view of the rest of the guests. One had his head down, eyes locked on the soft glow of his cell phone. Another was turned around chatting with her friend. Nearly everyone was talking and no one was paying any attention to the pre-show video screen which was showing a map with a slightly animated red line going from city to city.

Then, "ding," the universal airline signal that the pilot is about to speak.

"Hullo, and welcome to Soarin' Over California." came clearly from the speakers under the video screen. If somehow someone couldn't tell from the iconic deep voice, Patrick Warburton, in full pilot costume, appeared on the screen, introduced himself as Patrick, and continued the pre-show instructions.

Most Disneyland attractions have some form of pre-show instructions. Whether it's the foreboding voice of your disembodied ghost host of the Haunted Mansion saying, "Do not pull down on the safety bar please, I will lower it for you." or the cheery prospector of Thunder Mountain Railroad telling you to "Hold onto your hats and glasses folks! 'Cause this here's the wildest ride in the wilderness!" there is basic information that guests need to know. Judging by the number of hats one sees on the sides of the track on Thunder Mountain, many of those instructions go ignored!

In boarding gate C, however, nearly everyone's attention turned to the screen. The man's head lifted, no longer interested in whatever was on his phone seconds ago. The woman turned around, cutting off her conversation with her friend. In fact, no one was talking. The video had drawn everyone's attention.

Next came the same basic warnings as the other attractions but, thanks mostly to the delivery via video, it garnered much more focus.

"Soon, you will be airborne." Patrick announced. Wow, in that case, I *really* should pay attention. That sounds dangerous.

* * *

One of my favorite things about Commandment 4: Use a Wienie! is that it follows its own command. A wienie is a visual that draws in your audience's attention. Anyone glancing over Mickey's Ten Commandments will immediately be drawn to number 4 based on the wording alone. I know I was. The rest of the titles are simple and make sense, but the word wienie really stands out.

I've heard many origins for the term. One comes from Walt's old theater days. In order to get dogs to follow stage directions Walt would lead them around with a hot dog, literally a wienie. Sam Genneway, in *Disneyland Story*, says it was how Walt led his dog at home. I've also heard a less exciting explanation that it is simply slang from the silent film world. In any case, the wienie serves to guide your audience to where you want them to focus. In teacher-speak, it is pretty similar to the idea of an anticipatory set. It is the way we help our students focus on our specific content or the task at hand.

Disneyland's most famous wienie is the previously mentioned Sleeping Beauty's Castle. When you arrive at Disneyland's front gate most of the park is not visible because the elevated train tracks block your view. However, off in the distance, you can clearly see the pink walls and blue spires of the castle. (You can also see the Matterhorn mountain off to the side, but the castle is front and center.) The view of the castle entices you to go forward, through the entry tunnel and out onto Main Street, U.S.A. Once you're on Main Street the rest of the castle becomes visible and you are drawn further into the park. The park designers' use of perspective makes it appear as if the castle is far in the distance. A huge adventure awaits you! Everything else about the park may be a mystery, but you now have a goal in mind; See that castle up close. You head forward toward it (minus a couple stops of distraction to shop or eat) until you reach the central hub of the park.

At the hub, other wienies in the park pull you to your next destination. Off to the right you see the golden, futuristic spire of the Astro-orbiter at the entrance to Tomorrowland. Just to the left of that you see Matterhorn Mountain (which may have been the first wienie you saw if you drove in from the 5 Freeway) drawing you around the castle toward the rear of the park. To the left of the hub you see overgrown trees that only hint of what it is to come. If the wind is right, you might catch a glimpse of the Adventureland sign, but the mysterious trees are the true wienie for that land. Next to that you see a carved log wall of a fort introducing you to Frontierland. In each case, these big visual signposts draw you in.

While we may not be able to build large scale mountains or castles in our classrooms, we should not ignore the impact of physical objects like Sleeping Beauty's Castle and the Matterhorn. There is just something about having "real" objects. We certainly can't do it on Disneyland's scale, but we can still do it effectively.

One of my favorite physical classroom wienies is the locked box. It is my go-to tool any time my class is going to do a Breakout activity. A Breakout, which is really more of a break in, is a competition where students race to complete a series of puzzles to unlock a series of locks in a set amount of time.

It is like an escape room, but students are trying to get into the locked box instead of out of the room. A few days before the activity I place a large box in the front of the room with a bright red combination lock. Above the box I write "What's in the box? Find out in __ days." As I count down the days the students get more and more excited. They'll ask, "Can I try to guess?" and are shocked when I say, "Sure, go ahead." By the time the day of the lesson arrives they can't wait to do it. They are completely engaged before the lesson even starts. The lesson itself is engaging as well, but it involves a heavy amount of reading. They don't care. They are in. The wienie works!

In the book *Teach Like a Pirate,* Dave Burgess outlines some other ways to bring 3 dimensional wienies, or hooks as he calls them, into the classroom. One that I really like is called spotlight. He places a single object related to the day's lesson on a table in the front of the room. He turns off all the lights and puts a single spotlight on the object with a simple table lamp. That object draws in all the attention and gets kids thinking. He explains how you can take it even further by blacking out your walls and windows with plastic to further enhance the focus on the object.

That idea has grown into what are now known as room transformations. It is the idea of turning your classroom into another location. When you are at Disneyland the rest of the world seems to disappear. You are secluded from the huge freeway less than a mile away, the dozens of hotels towering all around you, and the very busy streets of Anaheim. A room transformation aims to do the same within the walls of your classroom. The room itself becomes the wienie. You can see great examples of this in professional escape rooms. I've seen rooms in office parks and strip malls remade into retro toy shops and spooky pirate ships. Some of the best examples of room transformations in education can be found at www. Setthestagetoengage.com. Here two teachers, Hope and Wade King, from the Ron Clark Academy showcase room transformations ranging from *Jurassic World* to *Harry Potter.* Their transformations are epic, far beyond what many of us will ever hope to do, but that doesn't mean we can't take a shot! It is, after all, as Walt Disney said, kind of fun to do the impossible.

My first attempt at a room transformation was a small one. When I did my first history mystery lab over 10 years ago I was inspired by an alternate reality game (ARG) called *Prototype 161* that I had played at a local gaming conference. One of the clues to the game was hidden in a corner of the conference floor that had been cordoned off with caution tape. It looked like something had smashed into the wall and left a mess of rubble on the floor. The caution tape kept most people away, but those who were in on the game knew the symbol on the wall indicated a clue was waiting nearby. It felt so awesome to lift the tape and investigate the scene like a forensics expert. I was in an enormous hall at the Los Angeles Convention Center but, for a brief moment, I left and was taken to a crime scene. I took this idea back to my classroom for an investigation into Julius Caesar's assassination. In one corner of the room, I drew a chalk outline of a body on the carpet. I added laminated photographs of physical evidence found at the scene and surrounded it all with caution tape. I placed a crumpled white sheet with splotches of red food coloring carefully inside the chalk outline. When students entered the room it immediately felt different. They were no longer in a classroom, they had been whisked away to Rome, 44 B.C.

While this was cool, and a technique I now use multiple times throughout the year, it wasn't really a complete transformation. I needed more than just one corner of the room. To "plus" my experience, I wanted to add sound to the mix. (The idea of "plussing" comes from Disney as well and will be discussed in depth in chapter 10: Keep it Up!) In my U.S. history class I have a lab where my students read first-hand accounts of life during the siege of Vicksburg in 1863. I arrange the desks to form "caves" and "trenches" that they must travel through as they seek out the readings. When the lab begins I shut off the lights since most citizens in Vicksburg dared not travel in the open during the day for fear of the constant artillery barrage, and project an old image of Vicksburg on the screen. I added sound in the form of random "booms" that would go off throughout the lab to accompany the flashes of white on the screen to simulate large artillery hits. Then, using a small bluetooth speaker which I hid under a desk, I played an audio track of crickets chirping to make it feel more like the night outdoors. At times throughout the lab that speaker plays the sound of footsteps crunching on dirt or a dog howling. Having it hidden among the students really helped the transformation. All of a sudden, the room sure felt a lot more like Vicksburg. This still, however, was not quite a full transformation. Everything outside the desks was still the classroom, albeit with the lights off.

For my most recent transformation I wanted to recreate the feeling of the Haunted Mansion attraction at Disneyland. I do a history mystery lab on Halloween each year where students investigate the cause of the spread of the Black Death. To turn it into The Haunted Classroom I put a giant red X on the outside of the classroom door to simulate the painted markings indicating a house under quarantine. Inside, I covered the windows with black butcher paper. I then put bright orange biohazard stickers on various objects throughout the room. I placed small, flickering, LED candles on each desk and around the various evidence stations in the room. With the room darkened it looked quite stunning. To add to the atmosphere I played a soundtrack of haunted house sounds accompanied by an eerie performance of *Ring Around the Rosie* by a young girl. To top it off I included the ultimate wienie, a live actor! I dressed as a plague doctor complete with a creepy bird mask. When I opened the door to the room the first thing the students saw was that mask and the soft glow of the LED candles. It was a powerful transformation that got them super excited to work and learn even though it was Halloween!

There are plenty of simple, cheap tricks we can use to transform our classroom. Glowing star stickers with crickets playing in the background can evoke a feeling of being outside at night. Blue tissue paper over the lights with the sound of soft bubbles makes the room feel like it is under water. Plastic tablecloths, silk plants and romantic music can turn your room into a bistro so common station activities become speed dating experiences your students will never forget. When your students walk into the classroom and see it transformed they are going to be immediately interested in what happens next.

Creating Digital Visual Magnets

Sometimes though physical wienies just aren't an option. Maybe you don't have your own classroom, your room decorations are defined for you or you are teaching online. Perhaps it simply a matter of not having enough time to put such a thing together. In such cases digital wienies, like the video instructions on Soarin' Over California, can fill the role well. Thanks to the Internet there are videos ready for just about any topic one can imagine. The key is to make sure the video is serving the right purpose, which is to draw attention. *Crash Course, BrainPOP* and *Khan Academy* videos are usually not good wienies! They are often good for instruction, but they don't become attention grabbing just by virtue of being a video. That may have worked 10 years ago, but not anymore. Know that your audience expects something more. They are very accustomed to tuning boring videos out!

A good video wienie should be no longer than three minutes and two is even better. Bob Gurr, remember, said we have only 15 seconds to engage them! The videos should be either visually stimulating or interesting in some other way such as through humor or mystery. Animated videos work great as they are different from most things students encounter in class. The video should be connected to the activity, but not necessarily instructional. They can be, of course, as in the Soarin' example, but the purpose in the classroom, most of the time, will be to build interest. Again, many such videos already exist on sites like YouTube and Netflix, just get searching!

The best videos though are the ones you make, or at least arrange, yourself. The first video wienies I made were movie-trailer style introductions for each of my units. They all follow the same formula. I open with the well-known green "preview" screen that precedes theatrical trailers. The music starts and a couple title cards serving as a text intro appear. With my Japan trailer, for example, students see "It was once our greatest enemy..." followed by "but is now one of our strongest allies." Then a unique title card with the name of the unit appears. The remainder of the video is just a series of short clips of the longer videos I will use in the PowerPoint presentations throughout the unit. I apply a unit-appropriate soundtrack and close with a "Coming Soon!" title card. Done! My students love these little introductions and they are so effective that I use them again at the end of the year as part of a review of the year's learning.

There are plenty of good video tools out there to make the creation process as easy as possible. Basic editing can be done for free on most computers using the open source program *OpenShot Video Editor*, while a more powerful editor like *Adobe Premiere* (my editor of choice) or *Sony Vegas* allow for much more detailed edits and effects like layering multiple sounds or video clips on top of one another. For making a trailer, *OpenShot* is plenty powerful. On the Mac side of things *iMovie* has a trailer-maker setting that makes things even easier. It does most of the process automatically and the results are spectacular. There is definitely a learning curve to any video editor, but it's nothing compared to building your own castle or mountain! You're a professional, I'm confident you can learn it.

No matter where your videos come from, how you present them is important. My favorite technique is to say nothing to introduce the video. I simply turn off the lights and click play. Nobody has to tell you to seek out Sleeping Beauty's Castle. The Soarin' introduction video doesn't start with a "please pay attention to the following" announcement. A good video wienie for the classroom, likewise, will speak for itself. There's nothing quite like a powerful soundtrack booming out of a dark room to grab attention.

From that starting point, I've gone much further in using videos as wienies. I have created video introductions for many of my labs and lessons and even for individual sections of my PowerPoints. My History Mystery labs, for example, each have an introduction themed after a different T.V. show. In each I mimic the colors and fonts of the show's true introduction and use the same soundtrack. I've created introductions based on *C.S.I., Law and Order, Pawn Stars, X-files* and more. They contain clips and credits just like the ones on TV. They help to set up the story organization for each investigation like we explored in the last chapter.

These videos work even better with celebrity involvement.

As I mentioned, the safety instructions for Soarin' for example are delivered by actor Patrick Warburton, known for his roles in *Seinfeld* and *Family Guy*. I'm sure you have plenty of celebrities in your contacts to ask to support your homemade classroom video so get to it! Oh, you don't? Well, neither do I. Thankfully, finding a sound-alike is surprisingly easy and affordable. The website *Fiverr* is a marketplace of creators who will perform small gigs for a low price, often as low as $5. If you go there and search for a celebrity voice, you'll almost certainly find what you're looking for. You pay your fee, send a script and have an audio file sent back to you within a few days. I've used a voice actor impersonating Liam Neeson from *Taken* for all my videos for *Fracture Crisis* and a Patrick Warburton sound alike for my own classroom welcome video. It adds a touch of excitement and reality that a soundtrack-only video just can't match. As soon as students hear that well-known voice their attention is drawn in even more deeply.

Depending on your level of technological skill, creating videos may sound intimidating and maybe impossible. Don't let that stop you! The Imagineers take on new challenges as a matter of course in their work, in fact, they invent them! Again, it is kind of fun to do the impossible. I never took a class on video editing. I just started doing it. There are tutorials available all over the Internet along with great videos on YouTube to teach you. You're a professional, you can do it!

That said, if you want to start with another type of wienie the Imagineers have got you covered. They use all sorts of media as wienies such as simple text and two-dimensional art, which makes sense for a company founded on animation. This art-as-wienie approach is best demonstrated in Disney's attraction posters found throughout the parks. They are teaser posters for various rides and attractions done in the style of movie posters.

In the early years of the park when you walked into the entrance plaza you did not see a line of people waiting to take a picture with a princess in front of the garden of flowers arranged in the shape of Mickey's head. Instead, you had a view of a low fence lined with attraction posters. This layout is shown in a shot in 2013's *Saving Mr. Banks*. In the film, modern Disneyland stands in for 1960s Disneyland and the best giveaway is the arrangement of the posters in front of the flowers. At that time the park needed these posters to build interest in the attractions because it was so new and nothing like it existed. These were the wienies that got people excited for the as-yet-unseen attractions to come. Today, images of the attractions are just a few keyboard clicks away. The same tease isn't as necessary. The posters still exist, but serve largely as flavor on the walls in the entrance tunnels as you exit the entrance plaza and transition into the first scene of the park – Main Street, U.S.A.

Despite having a less immediate purpose today these posters have become ubiquitous in Disney parks and marketing. Many of the posters have been archived in Daniel Handke and Vanessa Hunt's *Poster Art of the Disney Parks*. The book goes land by land throughout the Disney parks sharing these works of art. What stands out when one looks at so many in sequence is the huge variety of styles and techniques used in them. While many have the same art deco feel of the original Main Street, U.S.A posters it is important to remember that the style was used because the posters needed to fit on Main Street, U.S.A. (and to some extent due to the limits of color printing at the time.) A modern, computer-generated image would feel quite out of place on a street designed to invoke the early-mid 1900s. When one looks to more modern Disney parks, like Paris and Tokyo, many of the posters take on an equally modern feel. They look like any movie poster you'd find hanging in the lobby of your local theater today.

What if we treated our classroom lessons as upcoming attractions and presented them in movie poster style? Assuming we're following the other commandments, our lessons have many of the same elements of movies — adventure, excitement, mystery, etc. So, we can present them in the same way Hollywood presents their movies.

The first poster I made was for my History Mystery labs. I knew the vibe I wanted from the start. History Mystery labs are an opportunity for my students to role play as detectives. The iconic silhouette of Sherlock Holmes is the perfect visual representation. I added a brain colored in white to bring a little contrast to the design. I went with a dark red background as many of the labs involve assassinations. I sent the idea off to my brother who has a deep knowledge of film and he added some Hitchcock-style titling and I had my poster — almost. Something about it just felt off. Something was missing.

Most movie posters have what is known as a billing at the bottom. These text boxes with their iconic font-size changes provide information about the movie such as director, producer and lead actors. That's a definite no-no for a Disney attraction, however. Disney Imagineers, especially in the early days, did not take, or receive, personal credit for attractions. As Marty Sklar liked to remind others at Imagineering "There is only one name on the door at Walt Disney Imagineering." So, you won't find these billing lines on the Disney attraction posters. Still, I wanted to evoke the image of a movie poster in my students' minds immediately, so I decided to add one to my poster.

Since it would be rather silly to have just line after line of my name in a billing, as I am the director, producer, et al. in my classroom, I decided to use that text space to add short lesson descriptions. I still kept the alternating font size trope found in traditional movie poster billings by making any common words like "and" or "of" smaller in size than the more exciting words like "investigate" or "discover." I also added "actors" in the form of the historical figures we study in these labs such as Julius Caesar in the case of History Mystery. With the billing in place the poster was complete. It came out better than I dreamed, and I have since made many more for my other lesson types. I loved them so much I ended up creating more for individual lessons and even made teaser-style posters without a billing for each of my units throughout the year.

So, how do we make them? If you are a tech wizard, you'll want to use Photoshop as it does a great job of scaling images. If you are going to print your masterpiece at poster size, you'll need a very high resolution so that it doesn't come out looking pixelated. However, I'm not a tech wizard so I'll use the generic tool that works for all jobs — PowerPoint!

Step 1 — Set your canvas size. Standard movie posters are a slightly odd size. I recommend sizing your canvas at 3' by 2'. These dimensions are very close to a standard movie poster, are easier to find a frame for and, most importantly, are a standard size that can be printed at many online stores without additional charges. In PowerPoint click on the Design tab and then Slide Size. Choose Custom and set your width to 24 inches and your height to 36 inches.

It is important to work with a properly sized canvas so you can arrange your elements properly and get a good idea of how much an image will have to scale up to fit your canvas. Again, you don't want to scale up too much. The more you scale the less sharp your final poster will be.

Step 2 — Plan. What feeling are you going for? Excitement? Whimsy? Mystery? What movies exist with a similar feeling? What do the posters for those films look like? Can you borrow elements from those designs? What imagery helps to evoke that feeling? In Imagineering this is known as the Blue Sky phase of creation. Just aim as high as you can imagine. Get all the ideas down, then worry about logistics.

Step 3 — Gather your art. I am not good at creating art. I can't draw and, as I said, I'm not great with Photoshop. I have to rely on others for the art piece. My favorite site for this is Pixabay.com. Their images are completely free and come in very high resolutions. Many even come as vectors which are infinitely scalable so they will look good no matter how much you enlarge them.

Another option for art is to use your students. Especially at the high school level you likely have some talented young artists in your art or graphic design classes looking for an opportunity. They'll work cheap! Maybe you can swing some class credit for them. At the very least you can put their name on the final poster. They'll be thrilled to see their work valued in such a way. If they do hand-drawn artwork, you can easily scan it into your computer and use PowerPoint's background removal tool to clear out the white space, as long as they leave the background blank, leaving you with just the image you need.

Step 4 — Write the copy for your billing. Borrowing again from the Imagineers, I write a short lesson description using actions. This is not a learning objective. It is an attraction description! For example, the History Mystery poster billing reads: "Magical History Adventure presents an opportunity to investigate unsolved mysteries in history like a detective by examining artifacts, analyzing crime scenes and interviewing witnesses."

Step 5 — Arrange it all. This is where PowerPoint really shines. You can add titles and try out different fonts and colors. You can move things as much as you want and then easily return it to the previous position with a quick press of Control + Z to undo.

Step 6 — Create it! In PowerPoint, to turn your slide arrangement into a picture file you just click edit > select all then right click on the slide and select "Save as picture." If you're going to show your poster as a digital file, you're done. If you're going to print it you now have the file you'll need. One site I highly recommend for printing is Bingbanners.com. For a low price they'll print your poster on canvas which holds up great in class and well enough outside for short periods. They look great and will last far longer than a paper print. Your district might also have its own print shop which can cut down even further on costs.

Now display it. Remember, the idea is for the poster to serve as a wienie so if you can put it on an outside wall you'll have the best results. First impressions are important. We like to think that our students' first impression comes when they enter the room, but the truth is our outer walls tell a story too, and they often tell it first. For most of us that story is "nothing special to see here" as our walls look like any other in the school. If your wall was the one with lesson posters, what impression would that leave your students? I know how I felt as a kid every time that snowy peak of the Matterhorn showed up in the car window. That's the power of the wienie!

Turning Lesson Objectives into Visual Magnets

If that still sounds too daunting for you, then I suggest starting small with the easiest wienie, simple text. Disney Imagineers, in describing an attraction, always focus on the experience the guest will have, not the outcome, which is key. On the attractions page of the Disney website you can find these attraction descriptions. One such description reads "Cast off on a guided tour of the world's most remote rivers — where dangerous beasts and dry wit abound." Nowhere in Disneyland does one literally travel to the world's most remote rivers. In fact, one doesn't ever travel to a river at all (well, the Rivers of Americas I suppose...). There are also, in fact, no "dangerous beasts" on any attraction at the parks unless you count the feral cats that live in the trees between Soarin' and Grizzly River Run and even those are more adorable than dangerous.

The attraction, of course, is the world famous Jungle Cruise. In the attraction's narrative you begin your voyage in southeast Asia, continue on to the Nile in Africa then wrap up in South America's Amazon, all in just under six minutes. You do travel the world's most remote rivers! Along the journey guests encounter terrifying Bengal Tigers that jump up to 20 feet (but luckily the boat is 15 feet away so he'll just jump right over you), deadly hippos that show their intent to attack by blowing bubbles and wiggling their ears (which they just started doing), and a man-eating python (that is 3.14 meters long). You'll also see some of nature's most glorious offerings from walls of pure limestone (though many take it for granite) and the rarely seen backside of water (which, if you try to see at home will cause you to bang your head on the sink.)

Okay, so the dry wit part is there. One out of three on that description isn't bad!

Ignoring the narrative, what the guest actually does is get led like cattle to their seat on the boat. If they are placed in the middle row, they will suffer a lesser experience as their knees have no place to go. The skipper will open with a joke that 80% of the boat won't hear or pay attention to, 19% will not get, and will cause me to laugh. Guests will see the first animatronic, a bengal tiger that barely moves and is clearly made of plastic. Then there's some elephants followed by a scene in the veldt with some more clearly plastic looking animals that barely move (or don't at all.) Up comes the hippopotamus attack, which the skipper bravely fights off by firing a cap gun into the air, followed by more animatronics. Guests then see the 8th wonder of the world, the backside of water, pass by a few skulls, a snake, and Trader Sam (all again barely moving) before reaching the dock and leaving the attraction.

When explained that way it sounds awful, but *The Jungle Cruise* was Disneyland's most popular attraction in its opening years and, after a major revision a few years after the park opened to add humor to the experience, it has remained largely unchanged to this day. It is among my, and many enthusiasts favorite attractions. (My bucket list has only one item on it — lead the Jungle Cruise as a skipper.) It is the story and fantasy that matters, not the reality. If the attraction description were written accurately, it could read, "Guests pack into a slow-moving, track-guided boat with little to no leg room to see a bunch of animatronic animals while they pretend to travel around the world. By the end of the attraction guests will have heard many puns and jokes and have seen the backside of water." That is somewhat interesting, at least it offers jokes, but generally does not sound like an experience in which anyone would want to engage.

Sadly, that is pretty typical of the descriptions our students get for our classroom lessons. Often the only descriptions they get are when we are mandated to write the learning standard and objective on the board.

Here's an example of a standard from the California State standards that I've been required to post on my board:

> Describe the establishment by Constantine of the new capital in Constantinople and the development of the Byzantine Empire, with an emphasis on the consequences of the development of two distinct European civilizations, Eastern Orthodox and Roman Catholic, and their two distinct views on church-state relations.

My greatest hope when I post something like that is that my students see the boring text, quickly look away and never, ever read it. No good could come for a 7th grader trying to decipher that. It would likely turn them off from the subject with great malice. I felt awful just writing it!

Realizing these standards were rather ridiculous many schools started adding the objective to the board to make them more "student friendly." This led to such powerful goals as "Students will be able to define key terms about the Roman Empire." which I used in my class or "I can make inferences and draw conclusions about Greek and Roman artifacts from a primary source powerpoint." which I found on a website for an unidentified middle school. Many of us found this tedious and rather pointless as well which led to the birth of SWBAT — the acronym for "students will be able to." I've walked into many classes where I've seen a printed page with SWBAT taped to the white board next to a blank space where the rest of the objective could easily be written so it could be changed daily. Those five opening words were so pointless that we essentially eliminated them. Were the rest of the words in a learning objective any better? Only slightly. They were quite often very low cognitive level, comprehension-based verbs like define, locate or identify. None of which are particularly interesting mental challenges, nor are they typically much fun. I've sat through plenty of professional development training sessions and have personally not cared the slightest bit for the opening few minutes when the day's objectives are laid out. They are boring.

That said, I understand the reasoning behind sharing learning goals with students. As with many things in education the idea was good, the implementation was just, well... not. It is good for students to have a road map of where a particular lesson is going and a way to measure if they received what they should have from it. However, is that so important that we're willing to risk their interest in the lesson for it? I'm not. Not when it is so easy to do it in a much more exciting manner.

Look back at the description of the Jungle Cruise that Disney uses. It is active, involved and experiential. It sets up a narrative and provides an opening to a fantasy that makes the experience greater than what it really is. All that is done in just a couple lines of text. Any of us can do the same. So, wherever you list your assignment objectives whether it be on a class wall or on your class webpage, do it like the Imagineers!

When you do, you end up with lesson descriptions like "Explore the mountains of South America and discover the largest empire in Latin America." or "Investigate a mysterious document recently discovered in a dusty attic in Mexico. Who might have made it and what secrets does it contain?" These are examples of two assignment descriptions from my Latin America unit. The first activity is a lecture on the origins of the Inca. I could have written "SWBAT list geographic factors that influenced the early settlement of the Inca." Yawn. Exploring sounds way more interesting than listing and discovery is always fun. The second is a primary-source analysis of an Aztec Codex which could have "SWBAT determine the meaning of an Aztec primary source." as its learning objective. Yawn. Where are the remote rivers and dangerous animals? Where is the wienie?

This technique is remarkably easy and can be used with any lesson. Just start your description with an exciting verb and add fun and flavor from there. Even assessments can be made to sound interesting. They become a call to arms! "Battle against your toughest foe yet using all the skills and tactics you've gathered in the last month exploring Rome. Are you up to the challenge?" In math learning integers becomes "manipulate the forces of good and evil to determine the outcome of exciting conflicts." In English a poetry unit becomes "Judge a rap battle featuring some of history's sickest rhymes." Running laps? No! Your students are going to "Challenge yourself to overcome physical challenges to prepare for a zombie apocalypse."

Using an effective wienie helps us lead students to what happens next — learning. Visuals are a great way to draw students in, but their use does not stop there. We should continue to use them throughout the learning experience. Commandment 5 will teach us how!

Makin' Memories

Commandment 4: Use a Wienie

Create visual introductions to your lessons that engage students from the start and lead them through each major step.

* * *

What's This?

Visual introductions leave your students curious about what is to come. Out-of-the-ordinary objects or artwork can engage students in a lesson before the lesson even begins. Try a locked box or a spotlight on a unique artifact.

*What upcoming lesson do you have that
could open with a visual tease?**

Transformation

One of the goals of using a wienie is to help your students feel like a classroom isn't just a classroom. Transform it into a whole new location. Darken the windows, play some background music or project stars on the ceiling. Blow their minds!

*What simple tweaks could you make in your
classroom to feel like a new place?*

Un Poco Loco

This may sound crazy, but "students will be able to" isn't engaging. If our purpose is to introduce students to the lesson of the day, we should do so using language they will want to read and remember. Make it fun, make it exciting, make it an experience!

*Can you make a list of exciting action verbs
to have as go-tos for writing objectives?*

* * *

One Little Spark

"We needed what Walt Disney called a 'wienie' — the beckoning finger that says, "Come this way or you'll miss the fun.'"

—Marty Sklar

There's a Great Big Beautiful Tomorrow

Take your objective off the board. Rewrite it as an
active experience for your students. Use exciting
words like adventure, thrilling, and amazing.

CHAPTER FIVE

Communicate with Visual Literacy

"Make good use of color, shape, form, texture — all the nonverbal ways of communication."

—Marty Sklar, *Dream It! Do It!*

Walking under the raised railroad platform carrying a late 19th century steam engine and stepping out of the tunnel into Disneyland is quite the experience. Without any words of direction, you find yourself transported to early 20th century small-town America. To your left, City Hall with its flowing American flag atop its tallest spire towers above you. The marble columns, bright red brick facade and detailed trim scream "Victorian." At night, the globes of light that sit atop the light posts glow softly. There's no hint of the harsh, bright light of modern LED bulbs here. To your right, the Disneyland Opera House shares similar features, but adds decorative bunting rarely seen in modern design. Its entrance is flanked by two metal posts topped with classic hexagonal prism lamps creating what one could only really describe as "the old streetlamp shape."

The buildings dominate your view initially, but upon looking closer, the smaller visual details are just as evocative of the time period. The fire station, topped by a large bronze bell to signal danger, houses a bright red, horse-drawn cart. The walls display advertisements for old-timey bicycles with overly large front wheels. The marquee on the Main Street Cinema features white letters on a black background, the exact opposite of most you'd see today. Even the bright red paint, fanciful decorative swirls and carnival-like font of the popcorn cart bring on a feeling of nostalgia.

At the end of the street, as you fade into the central hub of the park, the details around you change, slowly and subtly, but just enough to let you know you are about to head into a new world. The changes in the pathways, fonts, colors and even the popcorn carts all make it clear you are on your way out of Main Street USA.

Thinking back, you may realize that nothing ever explicitly let you know you were there to begin with. There was no "Welcome to Mainstreet!" sign. There was no story introduction telling you to prepare to return to Walt's hometown of Marceline, Missouri and relive the typical American Main Street of the early 20th century. Nearly all the communication of time and place was done through visuals.

* * *

Many of the original Imagineers were people Walt Disney knew and worked with from the Disney animation studios. When he first set out to build the park, he spoke with an architect who told him that the only way he'd see his vision through was with people he knew and trusted. So, animators and writers with little to no formal engineering experience, were given the task of designing Disneyland. Not surprisingly, Disneyland became a visual tour-de-force. For a team experienced in creating visual art, it only made sense to design a park that reflected those skills. No traditional roller coasters or Ferris wheels here. Every attraction, storefront, pathway and even trashcan was designed with visuals in mind. Visuals tell a story and they communicate in ways that far too often we teachers don't consider.

The use of visual communication can be seen throughout Disneyland, not just on Main Street, U.S.A. One of my favorite examples is the title sign for The Jungle Cruise. It is a worn wooden sign with slightly cracking and fading paint implying age and a rustic feel. Beneath the text is a tribal mask with 4 spearheads pointing out like rays of the sun. Just beneath that art piece is another wooden sign reading "Tours Departing Daily." While there is definitely text, none of it directly tells the story. The visuals taken together certainly do. They give a feeling of adventure, mystery and danger. So much of the attraction's story is told in those few visuals.

Nowhere is this more effective than in the park's newest land, Galaxy's Edge. In many ways Galaxy's Edge does not feel like Disneyland. It feels like another world and it is due, in large part, to the use of visual communication. It begins with the entrance to the land. The "main" entrance, which was the only entrance for the first month of land's existence, is far in the back corner of the park beyond Critter Country. Guests make a very long trek along the Rivers of America down a long and winding dirt path walled in by rock formations on both sides. The rocks form a scene transition like one would find in a movie. One set of visuals slowly fades out while the other slowly fades in. Eventually the path opens and guests are immediately bom barded with Star Wars visuals — a crashed ship on your right and a moisture vaporator to your left (which just might be being worked on by Chewbacca!). The words "Star Wars" don't appear anywhere and that lack of textual communication continues throughout the land. The building signs, what there is of them anyway, are nearly all written in Aurebesh, the language of the Star Wars universe used in Batuu, not in English. Guests have to piece together where they are based on the visual clues.

It is the ultimate test of communicating with visual literacy and, I'll admit, it is quite jarring at first. I want to make a droid. Where is Droid Depot? Not surprisingly it is the shop near the beautifully sculpted droid models. Now I want to ride Millennium Falcon: Smuggler's Run. Where is that? Did you notice the enormous model of the Millennium Falcon? Yep, that's where you'll find it. We are accustomed to being spoon-fed all of our information, but leaving the guest to explore a little and discover through visual clues really drives home the experience of being in a far-off land in the Star Wars universe.

This type of communication happens all over the park. Think about Disneyland and try to visualize any directional signs in the park. Any luck? Probably not. Once you are inside Disneyland there are very few directional signs. While there are plenty of title signs on attractions, directional signs are just, by and large, not necessary. The visuals all around you tell you where you are and where you are going. In the few places where you do find them it is because the pathways are such that you can't see the visuals in the distance. The visuals tell the story!

Contrarily, Disneyland's closest competitor, Knott's Berry Farm, has directional signs as one of the first things one sees after passing through the front gate. Camp Snoopy this way, Silver Bullet that and Ghost Rider the other, all with arrows pointing the way. They do not allow the visuals to speak for themselves. As I noted before, this is for good reason. While there are some visual cues like the large statue of Snoopy wearing a ranger's hat sitting in a canoe at the entrance to Camp Snoopy, there isn't much else to differentiate one path from another. So, the signs are necessary (and still leave people lost!) The signage is a small thing, but it pulls you out of the immersion and makes Knott's feel less like a theme park and more like an amusement park. Explicit text just isn't as engaging as letting visuals tell the story.

Focusing on text communication also just doesn't make a ton of sense from a business perspective. Theme parks, especially Disneyland, serve an incredibly diverse population of customers. Disneyland has guests from all around the world speaking dozens, if not hundreds, of different languages. It would not be feasible to provide textual communication in all of those languages. It goes further, however. Not only does Disneyland have guests who can't read well in English, they have thousands of guests who can't read at all — kids! We often face similar spreads of abilities in our schools and classrooms. My school, for example, has students ranging in reading level from 1st all the way to 12th. These kids are frequently in the same class. As a result, some will do fine with an abundance of textual communication, but others will be left out. Designing using visual communication means all of your guests get to benefit.

However, in education, we love textual literacy, right? We are always trying to create "print rich environments." We do spelling and vocabulary tests. Text matters, doesn't it? Of course it does. We want that textual communication, however, to be effective. As Marty Sklar put it in *One Little Spark*, "To be an effective communicator make sure you take advantage of all the non-verbal tools you have at your command." As educators we don't talk nearly enough about effective presentation and communication. We might take one public speaking course in college (that's all I did) and maybe a literacy course in our teacher preparation programs, but rarely, if ever, are we taught how to put it all together. How do we blend effective presentations and instruction? We use all the non-verbal tools we possibly can — just like Imagineers!

One example of Imagineers using visual communication specifically to educate is found in the waiting area of Turtle Talk with Crush at Disney California Adventure. On the walls are huge, brightly colored, joyful drawings of characters from *Finding Nemo*. From the outside (the visually overwhelming Animation Academy hub) these characters draw the audience into the Crush attraction. Once inside you see that they've actually drawn you to much more. Along with the drawings there are text captions describing scientific information about each of them. These captions are rather lengthy, challenging (I vividly remember watching a young girl sounding out "primarily" as she read one of them and wanting to help her, you can't turn off teacher mode even at Disneyland!) and relatively uninteresting in comparison to the rest of Disneyland. In fact, they are (gasp!) educational. Yet, I see kids, regularly, reading them. The visuals tell the story that this is a fun, interesting box of text about sea creatures.

Let's try an experiment. Try to visualize a typical classroom presentation (PowerPoint, Keynote, or Slides, your pick!) What do you see? Most likely you see a slide with 3 to 4 bullet points, each with multiple lines of text. In the corner there is a somewhat random piece of clipart on a white background. Now click forward in your mind. Was there a transition? Probably not. Now you're on the next slide. What do you see? Most likely you see a slide with 3 to 4 bullet points, each with multiple lines of text. In the corner there is a somewhat random piece of clipart on a white background, but this time it is a different corner! Right?

Any time we are presenting content information to students we should be guiding them with visuals. Far too many times our presentations do not have any visual style to them. We often present 3 to 4 bullets of information in sentence form. Then we apply some default design pattern to the slides and assume we're done. We lecture from the slides, often reading the exact information that is written on them and then lament the fact that our students don't seem to be able to pay attention. Of course they aren't paying attention, the communication is too muddled.

For proof, you don't have to go far. To get an example I went on Google and did a search like many teachers would. I searched for "Election of 1824 PowerPoint" as it is one I had recently redone myself. I looked over the first few results. They were all pretty similar. They'd have their own quirks (such as one that has bubbles in the background of every slide for some reason), but generally you had the same format, style and information. I picked one to analyze in depth. Based on what I've seen in my years of teaching, and the other top search results, this is a good representation of what most presentations look like in history classes today.

The presentation begins with a title slide using a stock PowerPoint template in two colors; maroon and a brownish green which is as unpleasant to see as you'd think. The title, colored maroon in Times New Roman font reads "The Election of 1824." The subtitle, colored black in Arial, reads "Controversy leads to change. Was it for the better or worse?" Those would seem to imply some story organization. The next slide, which is all in Times New Roman has the title "Who is running?" followed by four bullet points listing the candidates. At the bottom of the page are 4 portraits without labels. One can reasonably assume they are of the candidates. They are sized equally vertically, but all are different widths. Two are black and white while two are in color. All 4 are very low resolution and there is clear pixelation on each. The next slide is just text with a title and 4 bullet points. They outline the "Corrupt Bargain", but are short and clearly would need to be expanded on orally by the teacher. The statements are only very loosely connected to one another. The next slide is a full screen map. It is low resolution and heavily pixelated. It shows the vote totals state by state for each candidate. It uses colors previously unused in the presentation and is filled with information. It is a clear violation of commandment 6, Avoid Overload.

Understanding that we are only seeing the visual and not

the accompanying lecture, the presentation seems flawed in many ways. The presentation has many more slides, but none vary from the structure of the first four. The viewer never sees the Arial font again and the potentially interesting story points from the title slide are never addressed. The bullet point "factoids" have little cohesion and seem to exist more as notes for the speaker than for the viewer. Every slide looks basically the same. Nothing stands out from anything else. There is very little interesting at which to look or with which to engage. In a classroom setting a teacher presenting such a show would likely lose student interest very quickly. It would take an incredibly dynamic speaker just to hold their attention beyond slide 4. Kids would likely copy down the words on the screen, but would just as likely process very little of it as they did. They'd put their notes away, go home and forget it all by the next day.

Unfortunately, presentations like this have led to a movement by some, primarily Grant Wiggins of *Understanding by Design* fame, to do away with lecture as a method of instruction entirely. I am the first to admit that bad lectures are bad teaching, but blaming the tool for the result makes little sense. If you put a wrench in my hands and ask me to fix... well, anything, it almost certainly will not happen. I am not skilled with hand tools. That doesn't mean people should stop using wrenches. It means either *I* should stop using them or learn how to use them properly. Lecture, or more appropriately storytelling, is how we humans have transferred knowledge for as long as history has been told. Remember, "it all starts with a story!" Lectures in school are often ineffective because they are a list of textual facts, not a visual story.

I don't blame the teachers for using or creating these presentations. Nobody taught us design skills when we were in our teacher preparation programs. Further, nearly every presentation we see in staff meetings or professional development programs looks just like the one described. Information is given to us non-visually all the time (and, let's be honest, we ignore a bunch of it!) so we don't have a model to work towards. Help us Imagineers!

When I attended the Courageous Creativity Conference,

a conference advocating for arts education held at the Disneyland Resort every summer, in 2018 there were multiple presentations given by current and retired Imagineers. I noticed immediately that their slides were almost completely devoid of text. Nearly every slide was just pictures. Every now and then there might be a title card with a word or two, but that was it. At the final presentation of the conference one of the presenters even apologized for one of her slides which included a quote because it had too much text. The slides were not particularly artistic. Most were just a photo or two on a simple background which supported the story being told. They didn't use any advanced animation techniques. Yet the presentations were extremely engaging.

Communicating with visuals puts a great emphasis on oral storytelling driving your presentation, since bulleted text cannot. The visuals don't work alone. They work in concert with one another to tell a complete story. Imagineer John Hench put it this way in *Designing Disney: Imagineering and the Art of the Show*, "When we design any area of a Disney park, we transform a *space* into a *story place*. Every element must work together to create an identity that supports the story of that place — structures, entrances and exits, walkways, landscaping, water elements and modes of transportation. Every element must in its form and color engage the guests' imagination and appeal to their emotions."

If we personalize this and change "area of a Disney park" to "presentation" and change the architectural references to lesson pieces (Bellwork, direct instruction, reading passages, etc.), we get quite the outline on how to design a great presentation. We also get an incredible challenge. As mentioned previously, few of us were taught presentation skills. Even fewer, I imagine, were taught color theory, visual composition or digital design. How are we to know what makes a good presentation when all we've ever seen are the standard "Title, 3 Bullets and Clipart" model? We can start by breaking down what we know doesn't work.

Consider the slide I described above. What are the visuals? How do they tie together? What is the story being told? Clearly the election of 1824, but that alone is not a story. It is a historical event that is little more than trivia, a fact to be memorized. This can work when your only aim is to get students to regurgitate facts on a multiple-choice test, but it doesn't work if you want them to retain learning long term. That's where story plays such an important role.

Creating your presentations to be story-telling aids isn't easy, but it is incredibly effective. So, how do we do it?

How to Create Visually Engaging Presentations

Step 1: Determine the key points of your story.

With any good story we need a setting, characters, and conflict. If you can't identify these three pieces, then your topic may not be the right one for a presentation. In math perhaps your story is the real-life problem behind the calculations. With science it can be the story of the first scientists to investigate a given topic or a modern-day example of that topic at work. In English and history we've got it easy and yet I constantly see us fall into the trap of memorization of facts. Our subjects are, or at least should be, completely built around story already. Facts are hard to remember, stories are easy.

In the case of the election of 1824, the characters are the four candidates and the new voters from the west. These new voters from the common class knew little about the machinations of the government. They would serve as a perfect stand-in for our students in the story as they often lack that knowledge as well. The best stories are those where the audience can easily identify with the protagonist. Some video games understand this so well that they seek to put you directly into the role by putting the game in first-person view. That's not easy to do in a classroom setting so finding a relatable character is even more important.

The setting shifts from the general election to the House of Representatives where the election is ultimately decided. The conflict is how intense and somewhat underhanded the competition among the four candidates was and how finally, the election was decided.

Those need to be the pieces of our story.

Step 2: Think about how to deliver your story visually.
The presidents, in this case, would be pretty easy to represent. They play themselves and not much of a larger role. Stock portraits will mostly be sufficient except that I really want to highlight Andrew Jackson's anger and frustration. For him I made three versions of his portrait. I started with the normal, expressionless portrait readily available through any image search. Using the program *CrazyTalk* I then made a version with him with an over-the-top smile and another with an angry scowl. So, instead of having a bullet point with "The corrupt bargain made Jackson and his supporters very angry." I have Jackson's portrait smile when I show him winning the popular vote and scowl when he ultimately loses the election. It is a strong, simple visual that students remember.

Representing the voters was a bit more of a challenge. How do you represent an entire group of people in a simple, visual style? I decided to create two characters based on an activity from Teacher Curriculum Institute's *History Alive*; one to represent the commoners, James McPoor, and another to represent the upper class, Alfred Weathybottom. I placed avatars for each, an overall wearing farmer and a top hat wearing banker respectively, in the bottom corner of each slide. As the presentation goes on the two characters comment on the events through speech bubbles. To visually represent their stereotypical personalities Farmer James' text is in all caps to show he is always excitedly, and inappropriately, yelling. Mr. Wealthybottom, (who always insists on being called Mr. Wealthybottom) "speaks" in a fancy cursive font with many big words. Nowhere do I describe the personalities of these characters, the visuals do the work. By the time the presentation is over, the students have a strong understanding of how the two groups viewed one another and why the election had become so contentious — far more so than if I had just put up a bullet point that read, "The election was contentious."

Step 3: Package it all together
The typical story, especially in film and theater has three acts, the set-up, the conflict and the resolution. This isn't always

easy, or even really possible, with some of our lessons. Finding a way to visually represent that story structure, even if it isn't directly connected to the lesson, helps build the feeling of story and helps with engagement and memory. In this case, I decided to represent this election as a game of *Super Smash Bros*, a party/fighting game from Nintendo. As a bit of parody, I titled the presentation *Super Smash Pres*. I took visual elements from the game and used them throughout the presentation.

For Act 1 I used the character select screen. It looks like a game of Super Smash Bros. except that the Nintendo characters are replaced by the 4 main candidates in the presidential race. From that opening screen it is clear to the audience that this was a battle, not just a typical election.

To represent the conflict I added a few animated graphs to show vote totals complete with farmer McPoor getting really excited when he sees Jackson win the popular and then the electoral votes. I also took a stage select screen straight out of *Super Smash Bros.* and made the chosen stage the House of Representatives. Again, this is far more memorable and effective as a teaching tool than a bullet point that reads "without a clear majority winner, the election was to be decided in the House of Representatives."

The story closes with Jackson's angry face, a very indignant Farmer McPoor and a "YOU WIN" screen with John Quincy Adams. I follow that with a very short bit of text to summarize the story, but otherwise the only text in the presentation are elements that enhance the story. There is no text just for the sake of facts to be copied down.

Designing your shows this way obviously takes more time than just typing in text and allowing PowerPoint to apply a design template, but it's worth it. When I started teaching, I thought my slides were better than others because I made sure to have at least one non-text visual on each slide. Looking back, those visuals were often irrelevant at best and distracting at worst. They were absolutely buried by the mountains of bulleted text. I was always frustrated that my students just mindlessly copied my notes from the screen no matter how much I begged them not to, but what else were they to do with such a presentation? There was no way they had time to process the amount of textual information on the screen (while also processing whatever I was saying at the time.) By focusing on using visual communication there isn't anything for them to copy! They have to process the information and then transfer it to their notes.

So, you're convinced that visual communication is important, but you're saying, "But I still don't know how." As I said, this is not something that we are trained in, or even have modeled for us, as teachers. That's okay, you can do this! You're a professional and you're creative! There are tons of great resources on design theory and how to use PowerPoint. For design, John Hench's *Designing Disney* is a great look into how and why the Imagineers arrange things visually as they do. Of course, you could also just go to Disneyland! Or, even better, head to Disney California Adventure. The Blue Sky Cellar there gives an inside look at Disney Imagineering. The exhibits change whenever new attractions or lands open in the park, but they always focus on design. The exhibit that accompanied the opening of Pixar Pier in 2018 offered *Imagineering Training Guide* worksheets for guests to complete with topics like environmental storytelling, color theory, and storytelling in an attraction. Not only are these worksheets, which can be found online, good examples of using visual communication themselves, the lessons they contain are a great guide to the process. While you won't find PowerPoint or Google Slides presentations in Disneyland to use as examples, you will get plenty of ideas for your own from the visual communication throughout the park.

Additionally, despite the overwhelming amount of subpar presentations out there, we do have plenty of examples of shows done right. TED Talks are a good example. When they use slides, they are limited and directly add to the story being told. The best examples though are the presentations from the late Steve Jobs of Apple. Starting with his iPhone introduction show in 2007 his presentations have stood out as unique and effective. I highly recommend going back and watching that presentation, which is available on YouTube. You will see very little text and lots of visuals. It is highly technical in spots and is introducing a product that few of us truly understood yet he takes us on a storied journey that by the end had consumers absolutely convinced they *had* to buy one. Carmine Gallo's *"The Presentation Secrets of Steve Jobs"* catalogues many of the techniques Jobs used to pull that off. Not surprisingly, the use of visuals is heavily emphasized. The Imagineers were ahead of the game!

We can, like in the case of the early Imagineers and their nods to animation, look to other communication industries for examples too. Magazines and graphic novels (also known as comic books) use visual literacy to get their ideas and stories across. As a kid I was never big into reading novels, but I was a voracious reader of magazines and comic books. I didn't dislike novels necessarily, but I loved the others. I've always been a daydreamer, so focusing on long passages of text didn't sit well with me. With magazines and comics, whenever my mind drifted it was to the visuals which I could easily bring to life in my mind. Ultimately, I almost certainly read more "words" than most kids, but I wanted the visual style offered in those media. That's why I've designed all of my presentations to look like magazines or comic books. I still get the same information across. I just make sure my dreamers have something to dream about!

With those big ideas out there let's get practical. Here are a few quick tips anyone can use right now to make their presentations less textual and more visual. The first is simple — pick the right font. If you look at the attraction signs at Disneyland, no two have the same font. You'll find similarities among the ones in the same land, such as the sharp edges and hard angles of the fonts in Tomorrowland or the whimsical curls and curves of those in Fantasyland, but each font speaks specifically to its own attraction. The other signs in the park are similarly themed to their land. Simple exit signs in Cars Land, for example, use rusted and oil-stained looking fonts to fit the story of living in a world built for automobiles.

There are near infinite choices of fonts available through websites like DaFont.com. Once downloaded and installed on your system they will pop up as font options in programs like *Word* and *Photoshop*. It is important to choose a font that fits your story. Far too often presenters just use either the stock font or a random instance of Comic Sans here and there. There should be a reason you choose what you choose. For example, in my Latin America unit each of the three native cultures we study has a unique font to help differentiate them in students' minds. The Mayan font looks like leafy vines over rocks because of their location in the jungle. The Aztec font has a horror feel to it alluding to their sacrifices, and the Inca font looks like carved stone because of their incredible architectural abilities. We can see again why the Imagineering idea that "it all starts with a story" is so true. If you don't have a story before you start designing, how will you even know what font to choose?

Not every bit of text in your presentation needs that fancy styling, just the main titles and a heading or two. Your main text should be simple and easy to read. Remember, it should only serve as a reference, not the focal point. You want it to blend into the overall image and nearly disappear from thought. I've experimented with textless presentations in the past and found that most of my students just aren't quite ready for that step so I've landed on limited, magazine-like captions in plain fonts like Arial to help them focus on the most important information.

Google Slides, unfortunately, is somewhat limited in font choices as you are limited to those built in by Google. If you do use Slides, you can always make your titles in PowerPoint, Photoshop or on a website like Cooltext.com and export them as images to be brought into Slides. It isn't the most elegant method, but it works.

The next tool is also not natively available in Slides (this is going to be a running theme.) It is the background removal tool in PowerPoint. The button to activate it is found in the upper-left corner any time you click on a picture you've inserted into your show. The tool does exactly what it says. It figures out (or tries to at least) what part of your picture is the background and deletes it leaving only the main figure or object. It is used primarily to remove the solid color background that often sits behind clipart. The tool isn't perfect and takes some effort depending on your initial image, but with even just a little effort the look of your slides improves greatly.

I cannot overstate how much better your slides will look when you remove that background (especially if it is a white one) from your images. It helps make your images look like they are part of a complete scene instead of just stand-alone, disconnected objects. Here's an example I made in just a few minutes.

Like with fonts you're not totally out of luck if you are a Slides user. Photoshop can remove backgrounds even more effectively than PowerPoint if you are willing to put up with the steep learning curve. There are also plenty of web tools and apps that do the same. Sites like RemoveBG (https://www.remove.bg/) are not quite as smooth as the tool in PowerPoint in my experience, but they work, and the results can be imported into Slides.

The final tool is one that I have not found any viable replacement for outside of PowerPoint and the Adobe Suite (specifically After Effects,) animation. First, most animation I see used in presentations is unnecessary and needlessly distracting. Few things are more frustrating as a listener than watching a presenter slow their speech in order to read along with their over-animated slide where each letter falls from the sky to fill a sentence. It isn't natural and it isn't effective. Animation is best when it is subtle. It is to draw attention to specific aspects of a presentation.

To animate an object in PowerPoint you select the object then click on the animation tab. You'll see a ton of animation options that you should promptly ignore. Without a specific reason to do otherwise one should not use any animation other than Fade. Our brains are accustomed to fades from movies and television. Any of the other options are jarring and unnatural. Once you've chosen you can then click on "Animation Pane" in the upper right. This will show your active animations on the current slide in a new column on the right. By right-clicking on the object name in that column you can change the parameters of the animation. PowerPoint and After Effects give you full control of all the aspects of animation — direction, speed, size and rotation. Again, these should only be changed if there is a specific reason to do so to help tell your story. Slides allows you to control some of these aspects, but only to a very limited degree. Learning to effectively manipulate animations can be a challenge, but one that can be overcome simply by playing around long enough!

Simplicity of animation is where PowerPoint really stands out as the presentation tool of choice. In 2016 Microsoft added the Morph tool to PowerPoint. For someone like myself who has spent literally hours on animations for a single slide this was an absolute game-changer. For those who don't have the time or skill to do so it is even more incredible. At its core the Morph tool is simple. It fills in the blanks between the start and end point of an animation. To use it you place an object (image or text) on a slide. You duplicate the slide by right-clicking on it in the left column and choosing Duplicate Slide. On the newly copied slide you move the object where you want it by clicking and dragging it into place. You then click on the Transitions tab at the top of the screen and select Morph. Done. That's it. Play your show and watch the magic happen! The tool fills in the frames of animation in between and smoothly moves, resizes, or rotates your object.

There is so much we can do as teachers with this tool outside of lecturing. The tool also works with changing object size and text colors. With a math problem specific lines and symbols can easily and smoothly be highlighted to emphasize process. In science, various cycle diagrams can visibly rotate on screen so students can really see that they end up back at the start each time. In history we can zoom in and out of specific points on maps to aid in telling our stories. In English Language Arts words can subtly appear or disappear to encourage reading for context or expanding word choice. The Morph tool is the only tool you'd need to pull off any of these animations. It is a simple and powerful tool with limitless options. Go play!

There are plenty of options available to us to increase our visual communication in the classroom. Modern technology has given us little excuse not to do it. If Disneyland can communicate key information to its vast audience, we can certainly do so for our students. Visuals are what make it possible.

Makin' Memories

Commandment 5: Communicate with Visual Literacy

Though text is important to education we should take advantage of the fact that a picture is worth a thousand words. Use color, fonts, and graphics to communicate whenever possible.

* * *

I Won't Say I'm In Love

PowerPoint unfairly gets a bad rap. It is a powerful tool that can greatly enhance our presentations. When you take some time to learn what it can do you will be amazed. I won't say I love PowerPoint, but it's close!

> *What's something cool you've seen done in PowerPoint that you could learn how to do by watching a tutorial on YouTube?*

Always Let Your Conscience be Your Guide

Visual communication needs to be built around a story. The story of your presentation should be like your conscience, not seen, but guiding everything you say and do. As you are designing a presentation keep asking yourself "what are these visuals communicating to my audience?" They may not hear, or understand, your words so make sure the visuals are sending the right message.

> *What do the visuals of your latest presentation communicate to your audience?*

Colors of the Wind

Color is a big part of communication that we often ignore. Don't just pick a random template and hope for the best. Consider what message your colors are sending. Ask yourself why your text is a certain color. Can't answer that? Go back to your story as your guide!

What color pairs look great to you (think about sports uniforms!) that you might use?

* * *

One Little Spark

"Our handbooks and training aids were always creative and interesting rather than the opposite which would be "dull and academic."

—Doug Lipp, Former Head of Disney University

There's a Great Big Beautiful Tomorrow

Create a welcome slide for your students. Use as few words as possible and definitely no bullet points! Use a background removal tool to take the white background out of the images you include. Use that slide to set the mood for your day's lesson.

CHAPTER SIX

Avoid Overload, Create Turn-ons

"Resist the temptation to overload your audience with too much information and too many objects."

—Marty Sklar, *Dream It! Do It!*

On a recent Disneyland trip I visited along with my aunt who, despite being a Southern California native, has lived in another state for many years and had not yet ridden the Indiana Jones Adventure attraction. It was the one thing she wanted to be sure to do on our visit. Only a couple months prior, I had ridden the attraction after a ten year or so break at the urging of my sister-in-law. I was quickly reminded why I had taken such a long break.

Still, not wanting my negative thoughts to influence my aunt, I told her I would gladly ride with her and wouldn't say anything about it to avoid spoiling anything. After our two and a half minutes of constant shaking and jerking about I asked, "Well?" She hesitated, collecting her thoughts. "It was fine. I just wish it didn't move so much." It clearly did not live up to her expectations. I could now explain to her why I don't think I'll be riding it again any time soon.

I don't particularly like The Indiana Jones Adventure attraction. I realize that confession may cause some to question my Disney fan credentials, but hear me out!

It has some spectacular effects, but the constant movement of the ride vehicle makes it hard to enjoy any of them. Thankfully, the final scene slows down to let you truly appreciate the experience. Your car slows to a stop and the attraction goes completely dark. As your car comes to a stop an animatronic Indy appears hanging from the ceiling with a flashlight. His light reveals a giant boulder slowly rolling toward him. Quickly you realize it is also rolling directly toward you! Your car sputters trying to restart as the boulder rolls ever closer. The engine finally turns over and you seemingly fly into reverse (spoiler alert, your car doesn't actually move backwards at all!) before lurching forward and diving down a path under the boulder. This fantastic scene highlights how much better the attraction would be if it just slowed down a bit.

While I may avoid it now, when the attraction opened in 1995 I couldn't wait to ride it. I heard so much about the ride portion of the attraction, but what really excited me was what I heard about the queue line. It's a good thing too as wait times often pushed well over two hours in those early years of the attraction. The queue line is filled with secret codes waiting to be deciphered. Guests would receive a decoder card to use throughout the line. I swear that somehow I had a decoder card before I went on the ride. I don't remember how I got it and maybe I'm remembering incorrectly, but even if that is the case it shows how much of an impact that decoder left on me. I vividly remember holding it up to every line of coded text on the walls as I waited in the line. I remember being startled when a wooden beam appeared to buckle and the stone ceiling above me began to collapse. While this is surely a frightening moment in any case it is all the more so when you are intensely focused on code breaking!

Upon entering the queue line you see a winding outdoor path. In this part of the line you see the first few messages to decode imprinted on shipping crates and, in one case, the cover of an old book. There are plenty of beautifully modeled tools which would be used on an archaeological dig. Meanwhile, an old-timey radio station plays in the background with news reports teasing the dangers of the temple to come.

At the end of the path you reach the entrance to the massive stone Temple of Mara. You step inside to a large, circular, room with a huge mural of the goddess Mara. You walk by an obelisk-shaped artifact and notice the holes in the wall that clearly must house poison-tipped darts just waiting to be fired. The path winds in such a way that you can only see a few feet ahead at any point. Beyond the next turn you see the first signs that you are in an on-going archaeological dig. The walls become encrusted with dirt and bamboo support poles strain under the weight of the roof above. The tunnels get tighter and tighter, further obscuring your view ahead, but completely in line with the story. Most importantly, you can't see the crowd in front of you or how long the line actually is.

Eventually the tunnel widens and you are presented with the ride introduction video. The pathway tightens once more before you finally reach the attraction loading area. That visual is stunning. It is hard to believe that something of such scope (and loud noises!) was so close to you that whole time.

For me, between hiding the queue and all the interactivity I barely noticed the wait. I was so engaged in the decoding, the traps and the incredible models that what should have overwhelmed me and caused frustration instead became the highlight!

Out of sight, out of mind!

* * *

The first 5 of Mickey's Commandments require little defense. They are clearly evident throughout Disneyland. Upon reading commandment 6, however, one might just experience a double take. Avoid overload? Didn't I say that my problem with Indiana Jones Adventure is that it has too much going on? Isn't Disneyland all about overload? Just consider Main Street, U.S.A. The second you walk in every one of your senses is bombarded. You smell (and probably soon taste!) popcorn. You hear music and the piercing whistle of the steam engines of the Disneyland Railroad. You feel the cobbled brick road on your feet. You see more than your eyes can possibly take in. Buildings of differ-ent sizes and shapes, brightly painted cars from different eras, lush trees and flowers that burst with colors you didn't think naturally possible. It would seem that with so much sensory stimulation you'd never have to leave that opening plaza or that perhaps to do so would just be far too overwhelming.

And yet... you continue on.

You are drawn further into the park where you experience humor in the Fantasyland Theater live retellings of *Tangled* and

Beauty and the Beast. You experience the unmatched thrills of diving through steep drops and tight turns in near total darkness as rock music blasts in your ears on Space Mountain. You experience the majesty of the nighttime fireworks and projection spectacular that turns Sleeping Beauty Castle into the largest screen you've ever seen. You experience the delicious first bite of that Monte Cristo sandwich from The Blue Bayou that is somehow, all at once, sweet, salty, crunchy, and smooth. The further you go the more your senses experience.

And yet, the guests demand more! More thrills, more shows and, of course, more food. Somehow the Imagineers found ways to bombard your senses at every step and leave you wanting more. The guests do not feel overwhelmed. They feel engaged and ready to take on whatever else Disneyland might offer.

Oh, if only our classrooms could be like that!

What do they do differently to make this work? As strange as it sounds, they simply avoid overload. They are masters of giving you just enough information at just the right time. Often they do this by simply hiding it. Each land is largely self-contained. In most cases, you can't see one land from inside of another. They keep your focus on one thing at a time. I also mentioned how they have tried to hide the most overwhelming aspect of a Disneyland trip — the lines. Space Mountain, which often runs the longest wait times in the park, does this brilliantly. When approaching the attraction, you rarely see anyone in line. They are there, trust me! Most of the line is up on a raised, walled platform not visible from the ground. More of it is housed inside the ride building itself. Only the very start of the line is visible. A few dozen people in line isn't overwhelming!

This is the one aspect of this commandment I do pretty well. I'm a huge fan of giving students just enough information to get them going on an activity and letting them go. I used to purposefully over-explain directions, but learned that as soon as I finished talking, no matter how well I explained it, I'd immediately get questions. I figure, avoid the overload, get them going quickly then take the questions as needed. It isn't flawless (the line for Space Mountain is still long after all), but it does get my students doing things they might not try otherwise!

Aside from that, avoiding overload is something with which I have personally struggled mightily throughout my career. I want to do something different every day. My colleagues often try to convince me to keep things simple. I just can't seem to do it! I have always been a fast learner and that has translated to my teaching. I tend to talk very fast when I teach. At first, I wore it as a badge of honor. I mean, after all, I am supposed to teach all of human history over the course of 1700 years in roughly 150 days. I have to go fast, right? Plus, I love history! I learned all this cool stuff in college, and they should get to learn it too. I let out many a satisfied sigh when I reached the end of my content the first few years. I did it! I taught it all! Well, I *said* it all. I'm not sure I taught much of anything looking back. I frequently overloaded my students, not with work, but simply with content. By asking them to learn everything they ended up learning close to nothing.

If only I had read Marty's book earlier. He opens the chapter on commandment 6 saying "Your first task on any new project is to learn as much as you can about the subjects of your story or assignment. Your second task is to become a great editor. Resist the temptation to overload your audience with everything you have learned, with too much information and too many objects."

Oops.

Marty was a writer at UCLA when he started at Disney. He continued writing while working for Disney when he created *The Disneyland News*. He also wrote many of Walt's most important speeches. Both of which required being concise. If anyone knew about editing, it was Marty. Keeping things short and to the point is key.

As a student of history, particularly in college, the overload came from the amount of text. I was often assigned so much reading that though I did it, I rarely remembered much from it. It got so bad that in my 3rd year I walked into one of my upper division history courses on the first day, saw a syllabus requiring us to read a full novel a week for 10 weeks, got up, walked out, and changed my major to economics! I still earned my history teaching certificate as I've long found the stories fascinating and loved the idea of sharing them with students. So, when I became a history teacher, I wanted to avoid using the textbook as much as possible.

Not knowing any other way, I replaced it with lectures. It was the very early days of PowerPoint and most teachers were still using overhead projectors and transparencies. It was so early that I ran my shows on a CRT television set, not a projector. There really wasn't any design model to follow. As a result, my early PowerPoint presentations were incredibly text heavy. I felt I had to have all the information in them that my kids wouldn't be seeing in their textbook. It worked well enough. My kids performed well on district assessments and they liked my class, at least in part because they weren't buried by the textbook. Still, I regularly saw those glazed over eyes indicating loss of focus and daydreaming. I was still overloading them with information.

After a few years of minor edits and trying to overcome the overload with more pictures, sounds and videos without much improvement I admitted I had to change things significantly. I sat down one summer with the goal of simplifying the text in my presentations. When I began the rewriting process, I was immediately struck by the weight of the task. I just had so much text. How could I decide what to cut? First to go was anything that didn't directly connect to the story I was trying to tell. That didn't work well.

I was able to eliminate some points entirely, but most I found myself unable to cut. I simply knew too much! The only way it was going to work was if I became a great, and merciless, editor. As someone with a passion for history that wouldn't be easy. It's an odd thing to consider that it might be easier to deliver simple information if you aren't passionate about it, but that certainly seems to be the case! For example, I often get the opportunity to teach math in small bursts. I like math, but I'm not passionate about it in the way I am with history. My AVID students get tutoring in their academic subjects twice a week and math comes up frequently. Usually, they work things out together, but sometimes they have to call me in to help. I do a short lesson with the goal of answering their specific difficulty. I don't plan anything. We just do it. Oftentimes kids will say things like "Why didn't my math teacher just explain it like that?" or "I wish you taught us math all the time." Well, no you don't. I simply don't know enough math to know what I don't know. That makes it very easy for me to edit things out and provide a short, precisely targeted lesson. It does not allow me to teach the breadth of math content in a logical manner. We have to know our content in depth, we just also have to be aware that sometimes we just know too much.

While trying to edit down my content I quickly realized that part of my problem was that I wasn't telling individual stories at all. "History" was my story and there's a whole lot of it to tell. I was just giving the textbook to my students in presentation form. Textbooks don't tell coherent stories (generally), they just provide facts in a loosely organized manner. Determined not to start over completely, I made do with what I had. Telling a story would have to come later (like perhaps in the next chapter!)

I had a conversation with a colleague about this problem and he said that he simplifies things for his students by color-coding his notes. Information that needed to be written was one color. Information that didn't was another. That would definitely reduce the overload. My next pass through my presentations then was to add a color-coded system. I landed on a stoplight themed system with each color having a different meaning. I used visual literacy! Red meant "Stop and copy exactly" which was used for key terms, quotes and names. Yellow meant "Slow down and rewrite" which was used for most background information and ended up being used most frequently. Green meant "Go on, you don't need to write this" and was used for any extra fun facts or things that I knew would not come up again in class. I should have realized immediately that green really meant "Mr. Roughton there is no reason for this to ever be on a screen if it isn't important," but I didn't.

The students liked the color-coded system and were doing more processing now with the yellow text in particular. I think this method is a good stopgap measure to use in a pinch, but I still wasn't happy. I noticed that the longer the year went on the more they resorted to just copying the yellow text verbatim. Upon analysis I realized that not only was I missing unifying stories, but by stripping the context out of my text on screen I had managed to even remove many of the individual stories behind the concepts I was teaching. Major swing and a miss.

Fine, we'll start from scratch after all. So, after retheming all of my units around a story, a process I'll explain in Chapter 7, I redesigned all my presentations with simplicity as my goal. It took me many years to realize that the problem with PowerPoint isn't PowerPoint. It is how we use it. PowerPoint, Slides and Keynote are presentation aids, they are not presentations in and of themselves. They should provide only those things that I the presenter cannot. (One of the things I cannot provide is a personal lecture for absent students so I do still include more text in my presentations for students than I would for a conference or workshop.) I also realized that though my goal of shortening my bullet points was a fine one, the real problem was the existence of the bullet points at all. Replacing a textbook doesn't mean making a slightly better textbook!

With the shackles of textbook-replacement broken I could now make my presentations look however I wanted. I could make them fun and simple. Consider the park maps at Disneyland. These maps provide a ton of information. They don't just show you the location of major attractions. They include every restaurant, shop and restroom as well. Plus, there are parade routes, restaurant menu summaries, indicators for FastPass eligibility, and about 20 other icons. All of this fits on one page! It could very easily feel overloaded, but it doesn't. Instead, it is an invitation to the magic that is about to happen in the park. Kids (and adults!) pick them up at the entry turnstiles and start studying them like great explorers!

The maps simplify the information in a few smart ways. First, everything is color coded by location. Each land has its own color highlight that matches the attraction descriptions. So, when one finds an attraction, shop or restaurant they want to visit they can easily find it on the map by looking for the accompanying color. Like nearly all maps, these have compass roses indicating direction but, in a nod to the importance of simplicity, the one on the map for California Adventure is "upside-down" with south at the top of the rose. If the map had kept the traditional up-is-north, down-is-south, then the park entrance would be at the top of the map and the park itself would appear upside-down instead of the compass rose. For Disney, simplicity is more important than fidelity. As a result, while the map does indeed hold a great deal of information, it is easily parsed and found when needed.

Secondly, the maps are fun! Remember, the commandment states, "Avoid Overload — create turn-ons." The maps are works of art with a very Disney feel. They have a cartoonish style to them as they are inked in bright colors. I vividly remember as a child imagining the thrill of Big Thunder Mountain as I traced its track route on the map. Even things that could feel like overload, such as the aforementioned compass rose, are made fun. The compass is shaped like Mickey Mouse's head to add a bit more whimsy. The maps are so enjoyable to view, in fact, that many were collected in a popular book *The Maps of the Disney Parks*. I've even seen them hung as art in people's homes. Well, *my* home, but still… great turn-on! Adding a touch of fun can make even the most complex documents less prone to overload. We'll focus on this particular aspect in Commandment 9 — For Every Ounce of Treatment, Add a Ton of Treat.

Finally, it is important to note what is *not* present on these maps. They do not have many common elements found on maps such as a scale, latitude lines or a legend. It would be wrong, however, to say that they are *missing* these elements. A legend explicitly stating "Pink means Fantasyland" is just not necessary. The Fantasyland label on the map is pink and so are all the pathways in that part of the park. Even a child could figure out that pink items are found in Fantasyland. Children often struggle with maps as they are an abstraction of reality. My students in particular struggle to understand how the scales work. They really can't grasp the concept of hundreds of miles anyway, so adding an additional layer of abstraction like "an inch is really a thousand miles" just doesn't work well for them. Disney wisely left the scale off their maps. There's no reason a guest needs to know exactly how far it is to walk to

Galaxy's Edge (it's surprisingly far)! One less piece of information and a bit less overload.

I decided to use a similar cartoon style for my slideshows. To give them a comic book feel, instead of having lines of bulleted text I created caption bubbles and boxes to house the text. By doing this the text is contained in its own small space leaving the visuals to carry the load. While in some cases my slides have more text now than they did originally, they *feel* far less overloaded. The text is interesting and tells a story. It is not a bulleted collection of disconnected facts. Students can read the caption text once through and be able to take notes from there. They won't need to read it over and over as they did with the previous, overloaded text. This format also has, by necessity, limited the number of points I make on each slide. It just doesn't make sense to put three loosely connected points into a single caption box. Truthfully, it doesn't make sense to put them into a single slide period, but the comic book design really drives it home.

Asking ourselves "What doesn't need to be here?" is a great way for us to simplify our slides, but it's also a great way to simplify our lessons and avoid overload. A couple years ago I went through this process with what had been one of my favorite activities, a Feudalism simulation I made based on one from Teacher's Curriculum Institute (TCI). In it each student is randomly assigned a role as a monarch, lord, knight or peasant. Each role has its own instruction sheet that must be followed step by step. It ends with a really fun moment where students build walls out of their desks to fend off an attack by a poorly costumed Viking (me.) If anyone isn't fulfilling their role, the lab doesn't work out properly, kind of like real Feudalism, but still frustrating. It has always been an exhausting activity for me to manage as I'm constantly on the move ensuring every role is completing every step, but because kids loved it so much I was willing to put up with it. Unfortunately, it got to the point where it just wasn't working with enough students for my effort to be worthwhile. Something had to change.

My first change, because I didn't know any better, was to double down on the overload, quite literally. I made another version of the lab based on Japanese Feudalism. I figured if

I was going to put the effort into teaching them how to run this simulation I might as well do it twice to get more bang for the buck. With previous experience the activity wouldn't feel nearly as overwhelming. The Japanese version is similar, but has its own unique twists, such as a ninja role that adds some excitement to the peasant classes. It worked out well and helped set up some good comparison discussions. However, it didn't solve the problems with the initial lab. Running that lab just got progressively more frustrating each time.

I felt like I was giving up, but I had to do something so finally, a few years ago, I skipped the lab for one of my more challenging classes. Instead, I did a very simple Feudalism simulation with cups of Skittles. Students still drew random roles, but they didn't do anything in those roles other than pay the class above them taxes. The kids got the idea that Feudalism was a top-down system built on birth not ability, but it wasn't nearly as memorable as the "full" version of the activity.

So, I decided to try to put the two versions together. I wanted the deep role-playing and fun of the original with the simplicity of the redo. The first step was to get rid of the individual instruction sheets. Not only was it a nightmare tracking the instructions for each step of the lab, it was annoying to pass out and collect the role sheets each period. Instead, I made one single sheet that just had general instructions for each role. This cut the instructions for each role down from an entire page to a couple sentences. The more detailed instructions for each step were moved to a PowerPoint presentation making them "on demand" right before they were needed instead of relying on each student to read and understand their steps for the entire activity up front.

Without having unique instruction sheets to hand out, I needed another way to randomly determine roles so I switched to playing cards. At first I planned to still have four manors (groups) and I'd divide them by suit. I realized though this just added unnecessary overload to the activity so I cut it down to two manors. Students either drew a red card and went to one side of the room or drew black and went to the other. It turns out that not only was this easier, but drawing cards is a lot more fun than being handed a piece of paper overloaded with text!

The activity had the same four roles and even added a 5th, monks, to represent the church's role in Feudalism. It starts very similarly with the monarch rising to take the throne while the rest clap and bow. He or she is given a plastic crown, a soda and chips to enjoy while everyone else toils away. The nobles manage Skittle collection along with the knights at their manors. The serfs must scoop Skittles one at a time from their central farm into their paper cup bucket. They must also hold onto one leg of their desk at all times to represent how they were bound to the land. This step was taken directly from the original TCI lab. Unlike many other parts of that lab it is easy to understand and helps show a point very clearly. After taxes are collected a viking (still me) attacks each manor, the castle and the church with paper balls. The knights defend their manors by using their textbooks as shields. Finally, a proper use for history textbooks!

It ended up working out great. The lab may be missing some of the "energy" from the original version, but calming each step down made it much easier to manage overload. The viking attack is no longer teased throughout the lab and is completely optional. If a class makes it through the steps quickly, I still do the attack, but it's no longer necessary. The promise of Skittles is more than enough to keep kids engaged throughout. More importantly, the kids still get the same learning out of the lab they did before. They really get how feudalism worked.

That is one of the keys to avoiding overload — providing just enough of the experience to get the story across. Marty uses the example of Peter Pan's Flight in his book. In the attraction you begin in the Darling house where you meet Peter and are encouraged by his "Here we gooooo!" You leave the house and see the spire of Big Ben below you as you fly over the London Bridge. Looking closely you don't see much else. There's a winding Thames river and some flat outlines of buildings, but none are recognizable. They might be accurate or they might not. I have no idea and it doesn't matter. The information provided is plenty to tell me this is London and I'm flying. That's what we want to do with our lessons. Get to the learning in a simple way. Start big and then edit down to just the necessary pieces (and maybe a piece or two of treat as well see in chapter 9!)

Another area where editing to limit overload is effective is in the reading passages we provide our students. Text complexity is a real barrier to comprehension for many of our students, and not just our English Learners. The evolution, or devolution as some see it, of language in the last few decades has left many of our students unable to comprehend historic, scientific and even many literary sources. According to a study by the Sunlight Foundation, even Congress members have lowered the text complexity of their speeches in recent years. When the average American adult reads at an 8th or 9th grade level expecting our students to comprehend the Constitution or Shakespeare's *Hamlet* without adjustments is a recipe for failure.

Sam Wineburg of Stanford's History Education Group has addressed this problem for years. In a 2012 article, *Text Complexity in the History Classroom,* he outlines the problem and a few solutions, all of which involve reducing overload. They are pose a central question, simplify the presentation and modify the text. Posing a central question is essentially organizing the reading around a story as we looked at in chapter 3. When reading has a purpose it is easier to comprehend.

We can take a few clues from Commandment 5, communicate with visual literacy, to help simplify the presentation of text with welcoming visuals and art. However, there are many other ways we can make the presentation of the text more inviting and less overwhelming. One simple technique that I learned the hard way is translating cursive handwriting into print. Years ago I put together an activity where students would read first-hand accounts of soldiers at Lexington and Concord. They'd read the letters and try to put together an hour-by-hour timeline of the events to help determine who was at fault for the conflict. I found the actual, hand-written letters on the Library of Congress website. The history couldn't be much more authentic. I chose fidelity over simplicity. The students divided into groups and received their letters. Almost immediately, I heard their complaints. "I can't read cursive!" "What does this one say?" "How about this one?" I bounced from group to group at an ever accelerating pace. After 30 minutes most groups hadn't gotten through even half of their first document. These kids had never been taught to read and write in cursive. They were definitely overloaded!

Unfamiliar writing style is, however, not the only way presentation of text leads to overload. The very layout and arrangement of the text can do it. Take the original U.S. Constitution. Not only is the writing in cursive, but it is very dense and in very long sentences. It is overwhelming just from a far-away glance. Students tasked with reading it may very well shut down before even trying just because of the intimidating structure. The same thing could happen with a technical document in science, a uniquely structured poem in English or a word problem in math.

In these cases, Wineburg recommends using larger fonts and wider line spacing to add white space to the text document. This is a great start. I've also found it useful to divide and number the paragraphs. "Chunking" the document into smaller pieces helps students see it in manageable parts instead of a single, over-loaded task. I also leave columns of white space on either side of the paragraphs to invite commentary, questions and analysis by students. By giving them ownership of the document they are, again, less likely to feel overloaded.

We can also provide typed versions of documents as opposed to asking our students to decode a script with which they are unfamiliar. Additionally, like with the Mickey shaped compass on the Disneyland map we can use simple graphics to make our documents more engaging and less overwhelming. I, for example, call all of my historical readings "HA!"s for "historical analysis." In the corner of each I have a small image of Nelson from *The Simpsons* along with a speech bubble and his trademark "ha ha!" It's a small thing, but when combined with other small changes makes for a much more appetizing task for students and makes them more willing to make an attempt to understand.

Redesigning documents in such a way doesn't only work for text. It can be very effective with graphics such as charts and artwork as well. Paintings, in particular, often provide far more information than our students realize. Students are often so overloaded by the little details that they ignore them completely. When I ask students to analyze a complex painting I do the same thing that I do with complex readings — I break it into chunks. I call this activity "Four Quarters." I mask off each quadrant of the painting and reveal them to students one by one. As each is revealed, students write a description of just that section. I ask them to try to include a detail no one else will notice. This focus helps reduce overload as they are not caught up in trying to describe every little thing, but instead focusing on finding that one best thing. Students then share out their descriptions and, invariably, they will start to guess what the full picture might represent. That was never my intent when I started using this strategy, but it almost makes it feel like a game and works to even further reduce the overload. This same strategy would work with maps, diagrams and charts from any subject.

While these strategies are a good start to reducing overload in any document they do not address what I feel is the biggest problem — text complexity. While there are different ways to measure it, the primary method is to count the number of words per sentence. In general, more words means more complexity. Long sentences imply long, multifaceted descriptions or discussions. They are just not easy to process and can definitely lead to overload. Here's an example. The first sentence of the Declaration of Independence reads:

> When in the Course of human events it becomes necessary for one people to dissolve the political bands which have connected them with another and to assume among the powers of the earth, the separate and equal station to which the Laws of Nature and of Nature's God entitle them, a decent respect to the opinions of mankind requires that they should declare the causes which impel them to the separation.

Yes, that's just the opening sentence!

We could find similar examples in technical documents or research papers in science along with any number of pieces of literature in our English courses. I remember "reading" William Shakespeare's *Romeo and Juliet* in 9th grade English and finding myself constantly lost due to the complexity level of the reading. I had similar experiences with Charles Dickens' *A Tale of Two Cities* and Joseph Conrad's *Heart of Darkness*. Those experiences soured me on reading in general. There was too much overload!

Cleaning up the presentation of those sources is a good start, but it is not going to allow the average 8th grader, or even the average adult, to decipher its meaning. Wineburg advocates for the seemingly radical step of rewriting the documents to fit the level of your students. This recommendation has faced criticism from some inside the history field for altering history (which is the ultimate no-no for a historian), but that argument comes up short when we consider the purpose of changing the documents. We want our students to be able to engage with these important texts. If we hold these documents as sacred, unchangeable texts, then we deprive our students of that opportunity. Interestingly, what is arguably the most sacred text in the Western world, the Bible, has been rewritten to reduce complexity and improve readability multiple times!

It is important, however, to do as little alteration of the text as possible. We do, after all, want to present the truth to our students. One option is to simply provide definitions for challenging words. These definitions can be placed right next to the word in the text. I've found limited success using this method. In my case, the students at my middle school, which includes 7th and 8th grade, have an average reading level hovering just below 4th grade. I have a very high proportion of English Learners. Providing the definitions isn't usually enough for them. They still tend to skip right over the words and just hope for the best. I need to modify the text to avoid overload.

One of my favorite tools for helping with the process is Rewordify.com. It isn't perfect, its base setting only suggests altering 3 words from the opening sentence of the Declaration for example, but it does a fairly good job of automatically lowering the text complexity of a passage of text. You can choose how it functions, either replacing words entirely or just providing the in text definition. You'll still need to do some work to ensure that the reading level is where your students need it to be and that the document remains true to its original intent. The key here is that it is okay to change the documents we want our students to read, analyze and evaluate.

If you have a lesson that cannot be modified or cut down, we can use other teaching tools to help reduce overload. In particular, cooperative learning, providing choice and using technology. Going back to my eye-opening failure with the Lexington and Concord lesson one thing that did impress me about my students was how diligent they were in trying to make it work. I have to credit that to the fact that I had them working cooperatively. Many of the groups were having a great time together trying to decipher this new language called "cursive." They laughed and giggled as they argued over literally individual letters at times. I've been to Disneyland alone. It's still great, but it does not compare to when I go with friends or family. Even the most difficult tasks feel less like overload when we get to work with others to tackle them.

Tasks can also feel less overloaded when we allow students to complete them using technology. This is, however, one adjustment we need to be wary of. If we aren't careful, the technology can serve to overload our audience even more than the task itself. Imagineer Joe Herrington said, "Technology is just one of our many tools. We, the Imagineers, are the master storytellers who must rein tech. The way a skilled horseman reins a spirited horse." He explains that though Disney is always pushing technology forward it must not overwhelm the story being told. In the education world, I frequently come across lessons where a certain piece of technology is the centerpiece, not the material. At the same time, I've seen far too many fad technology pieces come and go just in the last few years. (Many of which I've spent tons of time developing lessons for only to see them vanish into the ether!) We shouldn't just jump on a new technology platform because it seems cool. We need to ask ourselves if a particular tool is right for a particular job. Then we need to ask ourselves if requiring our students to use this tool will just make them feel overloaded.

Equally important, in my opinion, is the question of if we are setting them up to use a tool poorly. Adobe Spark is a relatively easy to use online video creation program that I really like. The user drops in video clips, text and images and it creates a music video-like final product. I've seen some amazing looking student work come out of it. I've also seen some awful looking student work come out of it. I've seen highly pixelated, blurry images that are half covered with a website's watermark. It is clear the student typed in the name of the topic and picked the first item that came up in Google Images. That's on us. We need to teach kids what it takes to use technology well. If that is going to take too much time and overload them then maybe we should pick a different tool. I'd note that despite my personal love of it, I've never had my students use Adobe Spark as an assignment. I'm trying to avoid overload.

So then, where does technology fit if we're trying to avoid overload? Frequently, in the hands of the teacher. While I firmly believe there are benefits to students using and creating with technology this is one of those areas where the teacher needs to be the expert. Technology should always be secondary to our content so it is up to us to know it well so our students can use it most effectively. Technology can help us present lessons on a specific path at different speeds to our students. It can also simplify the process of students recording and turning in answers. I've heard more than once that "digital worksheets are still worksheets." While that is true to an extent it ignores the fact that most of our students will feel like they are working far less when they fill in an online form than when they are writing out answers on a worksheet. That's the whole idea of avoiding overload. We don't want our students doing less or learning less. We just want them to *feel* like they are! Carefully used, reined in, technology can do just that.

These adjustments all help avoid overload and reduce stress on our students, but there is one part of school that overloads our students more than any other. It isn't reading and it isn't technology. It's the one part of school that commonly has its own form of anxiety attached — testing. So often students are trained to say "I'm just not a good test taker." when, in reality, the problem is that we have not practiced avoiding overload on our assessments. While we sadly can't do much to limit the overload of annual state testing there is plenty we can do for our own.

Step 1 is to ask yourself what you really want to measure. Early in my career I felt I had to measure everything. I made sure every vocabulary word and major topic had a question on the end of unit test. The tests were long and ultimately told me almost nothing. Students might do well or they might not. Regardless, in just a couple weeks, they'd forgotten most of the stuff on the test. I realized I was just measuring their ability to memorize trivia over a few week period. That's not why I became a teacher! Students groaned when I gave the tests and I felt the same myself. The test days were an utter waste. After much reflection I realized that what I really wanted to measure over the course of the year was my students' ability to use and apply history skills like detecting bias, evaluating reliability and determining key information from a source.

My assessments had to change. My first thought was to make my tests more authentic by using DBQs (Document Based Questions.) Students would analyze a series of documents and write a conclusion based on the information they contained. When my first DBQ stretched to the 3rd day of class and I still had students who hadn't finished I realized I messed up big time. My students were asked to write multi-step analyses for each document and then write a closing argumentative paragraph that ran a minimum of 10 sentences in order to have all the required parts. I absolutely had not avoided overload!

I did, however, love the discussions students were having during the test so I knew the idea was solid even if the execution was a failure. I decided to follow the simplification path. First, I cut down the number of documents to two. They didn't need to analyze four or five to demonstrate the skills. Next, I turned the written analysis question into multiple choice. For each document I asked two questions, what does this document show and what could a historian likely conclude based on this document? Then, students had a short answer question asking, "How does this document support the conclusion you chose in the question above?" Then, the final argumentative paragraph was broken down into individual sentences each with its own sentence frame. While it was still a 7-sentence paragraph, a great deal of the structural work was done for the students. They just had to do the historical thinking part, which is what I'm truly interested in measuring. Now even my kids who struggle to write paragraphs feel much less anxiety when facing my tests.

So, what have we learned? Avoiding overload does not mean expecting less from our students (or guests in Disney's case.) It doesn't mean holding back on extra touches of magic (like the music, Skittles and ridiculous hats). It means that our job, as Marty Sklar put it, is to be a great editor. We need to know what our kids need to learn or demonstrate and cut everything else out. The modified versions of my labs, presentations and tests are just as effective as the originals. In fact, they are much more streamlined which makes for a far better experience for me and for the students. I've still got a long way to go to avoid my tendency towards overload (as you may have felt from this long chapter!), but at least I now have a good example to follow.

Makin' Memories

Commandment 6: Avoid Overload, Create Turn-ons
We should limit how much we expect our students to learn in a given day. Make learning fun so we can teach more tomorrow!

* * *

Bare Necessities
In many ways the modern job of teacher has become curator. Our students have access to near-infinite information. We need to cut it down to that which is most necessary.

*When you look at your subject or state stan-
dards, what really matters most?*

Why Should I Worry?
Don't be afraid to reword and simplify reading passages. They aren't sacred. If the Bible can be simplified why should I worry about a historical passage?

*What reading(s) do your students struggle with
year after year that you could simplify?*

Let's Get Together
One way to avoid overload is to make tasks collaborative. Working together makes (almost) every task more enjoyable.

*What challenging tasks (or assessments) do you
use that could benefit from collaboration?*

* * *

One Little Spark

"What we're building here is just the spark...
what their imagination fills in after that, that's
the true genius of the original Disneyland."
—Scott Davis, Imagineer

There's a Great Big Beautiful Tomorrow

Simplify your reading passages for your students by
increasing the font size, adding more white space between
lines and providing in-text definitions for unfamiliar
words (or reword them entirely, it's okay, I swear!)

CHAPTER SEVEN

Tell One Story at a Time

"Stick to the story line; good stories are clear, logical and consistent."
—Marty Sklar, *Dream It! Do It!*

On June 12, 2019 I arrived at Disneyland for my reserved day in Galaxy's Edge. I excitedly received my wristband and joined the very large crowd outside of Galaxy's Edge. I huddled in the small bit of available shade and waited. In the background the sounds of exotic animals conjured up visions of intergalactic creatures traipsing through the trees. Next to me a young woman studied a book of phrases in Aurebesh. The excitement was palpable. Soon after a cheer erupted from the crowd in front of me. The cheer grew like a wave through the line.

The gates had opened. We were going in.

The crowd seemed sentient, like it knew where it was going. So, I followed. We walked across the entire land to the opposite side. I ended up in another incredibly long line though I knew not what for. It didn't matter, I was so caught up in the experience.

I approached a cast member to ask what I was waiting for. "Bright suns traveler!" they said. Well, okay then. It turned out it was for Oga's Cantina. I didn't care about that. I just wanted to ride the new attraction! I followed another, much smaller crowd, back towards where I started.

Along the way I heard the tell-tale sounds of spaceships zooming overhead. I saw cast members all dressed in Star Wars appropriate costumes. I felt the steam of the engine over the spit at Ronto's Roasters. I tasted... absolutely nothing because the blue milk line was a mile long and the menu at the restaurants looked disgusting, offering strange alien-sounding dishes like Fried Endorian Tip-yip and Yobshrimp Noodle Salad.

Every single detail helped tell the story of the land. I felt like a wayward traveler on a far-off planet because, for a few brief hours, I *was*.

As we left the land, my mom asked, "So, what did you think?" I didn't answer right away. It was unlike anything I'd ever experienced before. I definitely liked it, but I was still processing it all. It was live theater, different from anything else I'd experienced in Disneyland, just wait until you read about my experience with the storm troopers next chapter!

"I like it, though they clearly blew it with the food. How about you?"

"Well, I kind of thought it would have Luke and Han and characters like that. I don't really know this new stuff."

Hey, she's right. They built a *Star Wars* land without Luke and Leia! What were they thinking?!

* * *

In the summer of 2019 I read countless articles calling Star Wars: Galaxy's Edge a failure. The crowds at Disneyland were low that summer and some commentators jumped at the opportunity to blame Disney's newest land. Rarely, if ever, did they mention that Disney had blocked off significant numbers of their passholders (who are a large portion of the visitors to the California parks) and all their cast members from attending that summer specifically to cut down on the crowds. They also often neglected the fact that for the first month it was open only those with a reservation could get into Galaxy's Edge. The commentators largely blamed the low attendance on guests not being interested in Galaxy's Edge because it didn't feature the characters they knew and loved. No Luke. No Darth Vader. No Han Solo. No Leia. The problem with their analysis is that Galaxy's Edge itself was definitely crowded, even if the park itself wasn't (which, anecdotally, I also disagree with!) I visited Galaxy's Edge twice during the reservation period and was able to ride Smuggler's Run 7 times over those two visits with nearly no wait in the single rider line. I visited 3 more times that Summer after the reservation period and didn't see the wait under 80 minutes.

Still, why did the Imagineers make the decision not to include those classic characters? Simple. They know that the most successful experiences tell just one story at a time. Galaxy's Edge tells the story of Baatu, the furthest outpost in the galaxy. It has avoided most of the drama of the rest of the galaxy as the Imperial First Order has just arrived and set up shop. Its thriving rebel supporters occupy the other area of the land. Galaxy's Edge is the story of how these underequipped rebels resist the coming power of the empire. It is a new story with the guest as a key player. It is also the same general story of basically every Star Wars movie! Galaxy's Edge tells your story in the Star Wars universe. It isn't trying to tell Luke's story, that's a different one.

There are a few cameos from the old characters. The Millennium Falcon is parked right in the middle of the land, for example, and Chewbacca can often be seen walking around trying to fix the moisture vaporators. Baatu is a smuggler's paradise so it makes sense you'd see a ship known to belong to a series of smugglers. It doesn't make sense to see a bunch of Jedi walking around a far-off trading outpost. As I noted in chapter 5, Galaxy's Edge is the most immersive land Disney has created. Every cast member plays their own character with a unique backstory. There we talked about the visuals communicating a cohesive message. Every prop shows rust, wear and, sometimes, blaster marks. Here we see that maintaining a consistent story is another part of the magic.

The Imagineers take the story so seriously that even the merchandise available in the land fits it. There are few signs of the classic characters on any shirt, mug or other tchotchke, outside of R2-D2 who is a class of robot that would likely exist all around the galaxy. You won't even find the word Disney used in the land. If you want a souvenir that says "Galaxy's Edge" on it you'll have to get it in another land in the park! There is one story being told, Rebels vs. First Order, period. In a broader sense the story is that you are entering the world of Star Wars. Everything throughout the land must fit that story to avoid confusion.

Knott's Berry Farm down the freeway is a theme park with lands too. However, I struggle to name more than a couple. Can you name them? I've been to Knott's Berry Farm at least once a year for the last 20 years and I couldn't. I had to look up a map to find the names for all the lands. It has the western themed Ghost Town, the pier-like Boardwalk, the kid-friendly Camp Snoopy (I knew that one!) and a tribute to the Spanish heritage of California, Fiesta Village among others. The lands are not themed anywhere near the level of the lands of Disneyland which is why it is hard to identify them. Plus, they often do not tell one story, but many. Silver Bullet, arguably the park's most popular attraction, is a modern roller coaster. It sits between Calico Square and Fiesta Village. It doesn't seem to fit with either story except for the name sort of working. The same can be said for Sierra Sidewinder, a small twisting coaster found at the edge of Camp Snoopy and the very traditional carousel that sits in Fiesta Village.

I understand the difficulty Knott's faces. Whenever they want to add something new they have to find a place for it. The park is significantly smaller than Disneyland (57 acres versus 99 at Disneyland after the recently added 14 from Galaxy's Edge) and has little room to grow. To compete with Disneyland they have to keep new, big, exciting attractions coming. If those can't fit a particular theme, you just have to make them fit somewhere. In our classrooms we have strict limits as well. At the secondary level we get between 40 and 50 minutes in a given period and around 175 total teaching days in the year. In reality, we don't even get that much. Between days interrupted by assemblies, field trips, fire drills or other activities added with the fact that we really need most of our teaching done before state testing, which sometimes occurs more than a month before school lets out, and we're really looking at closer to 150 days. As I noted previously, Social Studies 7 in California has a ridiculous number of standards to teach. There are 13 units each with 6-12 sub points. When you're rushing to get through so much content it is very tempting to jam multiple stories into a period or even into a single activity.

While I still fall into this trap far more than I'd care to admit, in my early career it was a matter of course in my classroom. I'd been convinced by my education theory courses that kids couldn't pay attention to any one thing for more than 15 minutes which I thought meant I had to have a new activity ready at that time. (As an aside, I think that number is complete nonsense. I went to Disneyland with an 8-year-old who focused on plenty of things for more than 15 minutes including a Lego car that he worked on for nearly 45 before we adults stopped him so we could return to the park!) Thankfully, I've blocked most of those early years of teaching out of my memory, so I don't even remember how I attempted to do this impossible task. I do, however, remember that my classroom never seemed settled. Every time I transitioned from one task to another it was like starting class all over again. Starting around my 4th year, I worked hard to remove transitions from my classes. My class has been far more successful since. I didn't do so with any Disney tips in mind, I just simply realized that's where I was losing my kids. Now I know I was not telling one story at a time.

I talked about Carmine Gallo's *The Presentation Secrets of Steve Jobs* in chapter 5 and noted how he said a given story should not have more than three points. If my students' 6 teachers all followed this, then my kids would go home needing to remember 18 different points plus a countless number of social interactions in addition to whatever their parents asked them to do — and that's if we're doing it well! Typically, we are asking for much more than three in a given class. That sure is a lot to ask of a 12-year-old. I know I get frustrated when they come in and say they forgot to finish their work the night before, but maybe they really did forget. I surely have forgotten such things and I don't typically have 18 new things to remember each night. So, for their sake we need to make a sincere effort to stick to one story at a time.

So, how do we square the need to cover so much with the need to stick to one story? In Chapter 3 we looked at the commandment "Organize the flow of people and ideas" and learned that story is our organizational anchor. We looked at how we can have an overall narrative for our whole program and also for individual lessons. When we fully integrate those daily stories with the larger unit and ultimately class stories, we create a situation where we are telling one story at a time, but including many aspects of it. Going back to Star Wars as an example. The original Star Wars trilogy is Luke's story. Yet, there are large stretches in the movies where he basically disappears. For example, in *The Empire Strikes Back* we follow Han Solo and meet characters like Lando Calrissian and Jabba the Hutt and In *Return of the Jedi* we spend quite a bit of time on Endor meeting the Ewoks. Once we see how these stories ultimately play into Luke's, none of it seems out of place. We can teach plenty of stories as long as we make sure they fit into the overall theme of a unit.

When we don't, things can get ugly.

As I mentioned before, as part of my job as an AVID teacher I end up doing a lot of math instruction for my students. I started my education career in college as an AVID tutor where I spent four years tutoring high school math and one summer teaching it. While I do not have the ability to teach it as a class all day, I really enjoy math and helping my students with it. My struggle in doing so is often finding the right story to tell. Some units, such as ones on probability, lend themselves to stories easily. Others are a real stretch. Still, I love it. I love the concrete, right or wrong, nature of a math problem. I love that they are a series of puzzles to play with. I love math!

I tell you that because what I'm about to say might make math teachers a little upset. That is not my intent. This happens with every subject. It's just that many students suffer greatly when it comes to math at the middle level and beyond. The students at my school, on average, scored below standard on literally every math standard in grades 7 and 8 in 2018.

I think the biggest problem is that our math curriculum is telling far too many stories at once. The first unit of Math 7, for example, is, in part, about working with integers which Google defines as "a whole number, a number that is not a fraction." Essentially, the unit is about learning to work with negative numbers, but we emphasize the integers concept. Want to guess what the other part of the unit is? Yep, fractions. The very thing that Google defines as the opposite of integers!

Our teachers are in a bind. Fractions aren't really part of the unit. Kids were supposed to learn them in elementary school. Unfortunately, many of our kids come in with learning deficits, especially with fractions. If our teachers don't teach them early, they know it is going to cause difficulties later.

Teaching them together, however, has led to another serious difficulty. When subtracting integers our teachers teach our kids to use a method they call KCC — Keep, Change, Change.

Keep the first number as is, change the minus sign to a plus and change the sign on the last number to a negative. This alone is confusing for my students. I've seen them try using it on all sorts of problems without understanding why. When I ask what they are doing they proudly answer "KCC!" When I ask why they really don't know. They usually just say "it had a minus sign."

With a little digging I found at least part of the problem. It turns out that when teaching fractions, specifically dividing them, the teachers use a similarly named shortcut KCF — Keep, Change, Flip. In this case you keep the first fraction, change the division to multiplication and then flip the last fraction. Again, I've seen my kids misapply this rule over and over again. They end up flipping signs since the shortcut "Change" in KCC tells them to do so. A similar problem arises later in the year when they learn that to multiply fractions they can "cross cancel", but to solve equations with fractions they "cross multiply." There are just too many stories!

If instead we can tell one story at a time, we can eliminate some of this confusion. In the case of integers, the story I tell students is that everything they learned in elementary school about subtraction was a lie! They, in fact, CAN subtract big numbers from small numbers... well, except that subtraction doesn't even actually exist! Now, that's a fun story to talk about. All we actually do with integers is follow the order of operations and combine like terms. That is, of course, a massive oversimplification, but it works. Best of all, it keeps working throughout the class. The story doesn't change. As long as we're dealing with expressions without equal signs we can continue to follow order of operations and combine like terms. One story!

Of course, as I implied before, I'm quite guilty of violating this commandment with my history curriculum.

In 2019 my department attended a training that caused us to relook at our unit questions. In discussing our question for Rome — Overall, did the Roman Empire do more good or more bad? — one of my colleagues said with some exasperation, "I need to know what I'm actually teaching. What is the story?!" None of us had an answer, but we also didn't know how to fix it. We have very little time to teach Rome and it is expected that our students learned most of the story in 6th grade. In nearly

every case, they haven't. Narrowing 500 years of history down
to a story that fits into just a couple weeks is challenging at best.
That's why we made such a generic question for the unit. We
could basically teach anything about Rome in those two weeks
and kids could answer it. However, he was right. It didn't have a
single story which resulted in all of us teaching a bunch of seemingly random stories. In my own unit I jumped from Caesar's
assassination, to expansion through conquest, to architectural
achievements, to the beginning of Christianity, to a brief timeline of Roman empires including Diocletian dividing the empire
and Constantine moving the capital then ultimately to Rome's
fall. It was a whole bunch of stories without any real connection
other than they happened in Rome.

Then I saw a short video from Disney Imagineering about
theme and storytelling. Disney partnered with Khan Academy
to create a free series of short instructional videos for aspiring
design students called *Imagineering in a Box*. The video defined
the theme as "the unifying idea, the thing that the story is
about." It went on to say, "theme informs every aspect of a
story and the way it's told." That's what we were missing.

The recently developed C3 Framework for social studies
similarly encourages teachers to build their instruction
around what they term compelling questions. These questions
are not specifically content based. An article on the C3 website
describes them as "provocative, engaging, and worth spending
time on." They should also be at least somewhat "timeless,"
which is to say they include themes which are relevant today.
That sounds like the definition of a good story to me.

With these thoughts in mind, we made a very small change to
our question that gave it a whole new direction and allowed us to
tie the disparate topics into one narrative. We now ask, "What
were the three greatest achievements of the Romans?" The unit
theme is now legacy and the lasting impact of civilizations in
history. This works particularly well since I introduce my class
with the overall theme that it is our responsibility as modern
humans to pass on the legacy of those who came before us.

What's notable is that legacy was ostensibly already the
story we were telling in the Rome unit. We did name the
unit Foundations after all. Rome contributed mightily to the

development of Western history in government, language, religion and more. We built plenty of hooks into the unit that we knew we'd reference as the year went on. We treated it as the foundation of what was to come.

Unfortunately, when we made the change to the new title, we also kept much of the previous material that was in the unit and that's where the frustration came in. The opening story I told, for example, was the assassination of Julius Caesar and the following rise of Augustus. It's a great story full of action and betrayal. On its own it's exactly the kind of story I want to use to engage my students. However, in the context of the unit itself it just doesn't really fit. There isn't any follow up to the story and it doesn't play much of a part in the assessment either. I jumped from there into an exploration of Roman building projects and from there to the start of Christianity. It was all Roman, but that's about all the topics had in common.

The problem was largely one of increasing bloat. As I created new lessons over the years, I was hesitant to remove them even when they didn't fit the story. I had plenty of other similar one-off stories like the eruption of Mount Vesuvius and how the Romans could perform eye surgery as well. They were all individually engaging stories, but taken together the story of Rome just became a hodgepodge of events, inventions and people that just didn't make sense. I was definitely not telling one story at a time.

Imagineer Joe Rohde says in the *Imagineering in a Box* video, "the question you are always asking yourself is, 'Does this thing, or does it not, help feed into the theme?'" That has absolutely not been the question I have kept in mind while I've built my class over the years. In fact, I can't even say I've had one question in mind. I've had many. "Does this lesson look fun?" "Will this lesson fill up the empty spot I have in my calendar?" "Does this lesson use inquiry?" "Is it about topic x, y or z?" The list could go on. Those questions are fine to ask (except maybe the calendar one), but they should all come after first asking "Does this lesson or does it not help feed into the theme of my unit or my classroom?" If not, it almost certainly should not be pursued further.

Additionally, if you do come to your theme after having developed your lessons and units as I did then you have to realize that you are likely going to need new lessons to really drive home that theme. When you do add those new lessons sometimes the old has to go to make way for the new, especially if those older lessons don't fit the theme quite as well.

Giving up the old is sometimes very difficult. Imagineers regularly have to balance the desire of some guests to hold onto nostalgic attractions from their youth while bringing in modern ones to better fit their themes. Any time the slightest change happens you find people getting upset. When Soarin' Over California became Soarin' Over the World plenty of long-time Disney guests complained. When Soarin' Over California came back for a couple of months in the summer of 2019, I read multiple posts on forums and blogs begging Disney to keep it that way forever. One of my favorites went scene by scene critiquing the World version. The main complaint was how curved the Eiffel Tower appeared in the Paris scene. Having not experienced the California version in a few years I saw the point. Due to the curvature of the screen the Eiffel Tower *is* very curved, especially if you get a seat off to the side of the attraction. I didn't remember that from any scene in California and, clearly, neither did the author of the post.

Then I re-rode the California version of the attraction and quickly realized why I never noticed any of the scenes standing out as having curved images. It is because they *all* have curved images! While some, like the Golden Gate Bridge scene, show extreme amounts of curvature, none stand out because it happens throughout the entire attraction. Clearly the technology and techniques used to film the original version improved greatly in the few years that passed before Soarin' Over the World came along if it is only the Paris scene that now stands out! We have to be willing to get rid of our old lessons, as hard as it may be, to make room for new and improved ones that better tell our story.

While it is important to have an entire unit telling one story, we should also apply this commandment on a smaller scale to individual activities. Once you've organized the flow of your lesson through story it is important to ensure everything fits it in an orderly fashion. One example of this is my Christendom Culture Shock activity. Culture Shocks are a collection of mini activities designed to help students experience life in a civilization from the past. This particular one has been in my class rotation for over 10 years now. When I first built it I really didn't have a story to go with it. I simply wanted to get kids to experience various bits of daily life in Europe following the fall of Rome. The activities included ranking survival needs in a zombie apocalypse, shucking pea pods, building card houses, listening to medieval music and taking a Cosmo-style quiz on what type of leader a student would be.

Over the years I made some adjustments. The pea pods proved to be way too much work on my part and were replaced with pictures of pottage, the staple food of Christendom, from around the world today. I also added an activity about copying manuscript pages like monks did and another where students analyzed a painting of a medieval butcher shop. While all the activities tied directly to a concept we were learning about in Medieval Europe they did not really link to one another.

There was also no real sense of order. I started with the apocalypse one, which made sense given that we were transitioning from the order of Rome to the chaos of the early Dark ages. I then went into building card houses followed by the Cosmo Quiz. I then did the manuscript activity followed by the picture analysis before closing with the look at pottage and listening to the music if time permitted. I arranged them, for the most part, based on the order I created them. I just added more on to the end as I came up with them. Later I moved some around to ensure the most important ones came first in case we ran short on time. The leadership activity was pushed toward the end before ultimately being removed for time, along with the music activity.

Even with the disconnect the lab has been good. Kids enjoyed it and some learning certainly happened. It, however, was often quickly forgotten. While I used some of the activities as references for later learning it mostly just faded away as the unit went on. Of course it did. It didn't tell a single story. It told a bunch of little stories that just didn't last. So, in 2018, I decided to build it into a story. Luckily, I didn't have to build any more activities. I still start with the apocalypse idea. I now make sure that out of the 5 things the students say they'd need to get in an apocalypse they include food, water and shelter. I tell them the first priority is water. I ask them how people in Rome got their water before Rome fell (aqueducts.) I then point out that as the aqueducts broke down there wasn't anyone left to repair them so many people left the towns to move closer to rivers to access water. That's a story!

Now they've left the town and have their water. Next comes their food. We go over the incredibly disgusting pictures of pottage and I ask students which one they'd eat if they had to pick. I want them to start to feel the difficulty of living in this environment. Once they have food, they need shelter of course so I do the card house challenge. They typically fail miserably. I point out, again, the one story of how difficult it was to make this transition away from the Roman empire as they provided housing for many people previously.

Now that students are sufficiently convinced that this was a rough time to be alive, I point out that the only escape for low class peasants was to become a monk in the church. This improved their condition, but their lives still had challenges. This is where the manuscript copying activity comes in. The students also find this task to be nearly impossible and are just about ready to give up on survival. That's when I close with the analysis of the butcher shop painting. I point out that it wasn't all bad for everyone. While there was a massive lower class, about 10% of the population were nobility. They had access to nicer clothes and better diets. I tell them that tomorrow's presentation will focus on this part of society.

With very minimal changes the activity is now much more effective. It is now the story of transitioning from the rule of the Romans to the necessity of self-sufficiency in the Early Middle Ages. It transitions from the first presentation of the unit which focuses on how the church filled the leadership vacuum left by the loss of the Romans in the eyes of the peasant class to the rising power of the kings in the second presentation. Instead of just having this one-off, fun lesson I have a solid piece of the unit and that's specifically because it now tells one story at a time instead of 5!

But if every unit and lesson have their own story doesn't that put us right back where we started — telling too many stories at once? Hopefully not. Commandment 7 demands that the story hold fidelity throughout the experience.

Disneyland is a massive collection of stories. As we saw earlier every attraction, shop, show and restaurant has a unique story. However, that tells only a small part of the, well, story. There are the additional stories of each labor division at the park. Some are providing safety, others entertainment, and some are just there to ensure the day flows smoothly. They are all unique and it's a good thing! You wouldn't want the food services division to tell the story of a stomach-churning adventure — we'll leave that to the Imagineers! Then, of course, there are the individual stories of birthdays, weddings and first visits being told among the guests on a daily basis.

What then is *the* story of Disneyland? It's that story that Walt envisioned sitting on that bench so many decades ago — kids and adults should experience joy together. Every other story is not just subordinate to this one, but must be a part of it.

We'll look at the story of my classroom in depth in chapter 8, but start thinking about *the* story of your classroom.

Once you have your story the best way to ensure that you stick to it is careful planning. Every project at Walt Disney Imagineering is planned meticulously. Most begin as storyboards calling back to Walt's origins as an animator. Projects go through multiple stages of planning and most never get any further than that. There are countless projects that never saw their way to completion.

As educators we are taught very little about planning. Likely in our education courses we were taught how to do lesson plans of one type or another. If your program was anything like mine, that instruction was little more than how to fill out sections on a form. Anticipatory set? Check. Individual instruction? Check. Check for understanding? Check. Lesson done. I was never asked to truly consider how that lesson fit into an overall unit or story. In fact, the most commonly used lesson plan, the Madeline Hunter plan, rarely has any mention of the unit for which the lesson is designed outside of perhaps a state standard.

We ought to look at our lessons in a larger context. While individual lesson plans certainly have a place, especially early in one's career, unit plans are far more important than we typically believe. This is where the concept of storyboarding can help. I layout my lessons in blocks in the same manner — my blocks just happen to be digital. I do my unit plans using Google Calendar. It allows me to drop items into a given day then easily drag them to another if I want to make any changes, which I almost always do. I start with a rough idea of specific lessons and topics and rearrange them as I go to best fit my story. When I'm done, I can see the entire lesson from introduction to assessment. I can easily spot potential holes in the story or where two lessons that are on consecutive days just don't really fit together. At that point they are either easily moved or I can focus on building a better transition and clearer link to the story between them.

There are dozens of ways to plan and I don't believe one is necessarily better than another, but planning needs to happen. I know we are busy and planning is often something we think we can do without. As long as I have a lesson ready to go by 8:55 AM I'm good enough, right? Not quite. Far too often we fall into that trap and it leads us to lose our story. Our story isn't "I need to fill 50 minutes with some kind of learning today." We have to do better.

The final level of story takes us back to the beginning. I opened the chapter describing how everything in Disneyland must fit the same story. Each attraction must tell a story that fits its land and the land must tell its own story consistently, but they must also all tell the story of the park itself. Likewise, our units need to fit our classroom story and our classroom story needs to fit the overall vision or mission of our school. Define your story, plan it out and stick to it!

Makin' Memories

Commandment 7: Tell one story at a time

Everything in your classroom should fit your story. Anything that doesn't fit should go. Nothing should be done just to do it.

* * *

We Belong Together

Every lesson you plan should fit your unit or class theme. Making sure our lessons belong together is the best way to avoid our units getting too bloated as we add to them each year.

How do the lessons in your next unit fit together?

Let it Go

Anything that doesn't fit your theme should go. Even Disney has to remove old attractions so new ones can come in. It's hard to get rid of those old favorites, but nothing should be done just to do it.

What lesson have you done for years that just doesn't fit any more?

How Far I'll Go

The best way to stick to a story is to plan ahead. When we're rushed to get a lesson in front of our students we tend to compromise, and story is often ignored. Looking ahead ensures that every turn you take, every trail you track leads you back to your story.

Can you plan your next unit (or next week) ahead of schedule?

* * *

One Little Spark

"Our best stories are the ones that have a parallel universe — something guests can relate to."

—Kevin Rafferty, Imagineer

There's a Great Big Beautiful Tomorrow

Write a one sentence summary of the theme of your current unit for yourself. Keep that theme in mind as you plan the rest of the unit. Anything that doesn't fit the theme should go!

CHAPTER EIGHT

Avoid Contradictions — Maintain Identity

"Details in design or content that contradict one another confuse an audience about your story or the time period it takes place in."

—Marty Sklar, *Dream It! Do It!*

The crowd parted as a black-clad First Order Lieutenant, flanked by two armed Stormtroopers, marched past Droid Depot. Unfortunately, I didn't see them in time. My eyes were looking down at my map when the Lieutenant sternly commanded me to step aside. I looked up and nearly froze.

It wasn't my first time seeing Imperial troops accost a guest. Just a few months prior I stood by helplessly as my younger brother was pulled out of our group by two stormtroopers and challenged for his choice of T-shirt. Apparently, in Tomorrowland canon Buzz Lightyear is the sworn enemy of the Empire. He survived the encounter, no thanks to me.

This time I was alone, and I was not in Tomorrowland. I was in Galaxy's Edge. Perhaps more accurately I was in Baatu, a dusty trading post at the furthest edge of the Galaxy where the First Order had only minimal control and the rebels had begun to gather a small force. There were no signs of happy, Disney characters to remind me I was in the Magic Kingdom. Every object, sound and smell pointed to just one conclusion — I was no longer a guest. I was a citizen of Baatu and I had to think fast.

"Oh, I'm a supporter! Look at my shirt!" I said as I frantically pointed to the animated Stormtrooper, complete with "pew pew" onomatopoeia sound effects printed at the end of its blaster, on my shirt. "I'm one of you. I love the First Order!"

"If you were a true supporter, you would have moved imme-diately when I commanded you. Now step aside." came the reply from the Lieutenant with clear annoyance. Well... uh... I can't argue with that. "I'm sorry sir." I whispered as I clasped my hands together in front of my chest and bowed, half in respect and half as a prayer, while slowly backing away.

When I was sure they had passed I lifted my head. Only then did I ask myself, "What the heck just happened? Why did I just bow to a guy in a costume?!"

I smiled realizing I had been completely sucked in. Every visual and sound of Galaxy's Edge was so dedicated to fueling immersion that I was ready to be made a fool. The dedication with which the cast members played their characters had me convinced I was in a far-off outpost in the Star Wars universe about to be imprisoned for my lack of decorum.

By way of confession, not only is this rather embarrassing story 100% true, it happened again shortly after. A few weeks later I was approached again. This time I was playing with the Star Wars Data Pad app on my phone. The two stormtroopers "read the signals from my communicator" and challenged my loyalties. I again begged for my life! That's the power of authenticity.

* * *

My main piece of advice I give to all new and prospective teach-ers is simple and not one they typically hear in their education programs. Be yourself — always. Little did I know I was preach-ing Imagineering gospel! Everyone responds better to people they like and it's hard to like someone you perceive as fake. Van France in his memoir *Window on Main Street* said of Walt, "All of our people identified with Walt Disney. You might even think everyone knew him personally. Our guests also identified with him. The question most frequently asked by our visiting guests was, 'Is Walt Disney in the park today?'" Isn't that what we want from our students? Don't we want them disappointed when they have a substitute teacher instead of cheering? If we can be ourselves without contradiction, we can get there!

After reading many books about Walt Disney it is striking how consistent every person's perception of him was. I keep waiting to read a biography with a different viewpoint, but it hasn't happened yet. He was who he was, and he demanded consistency not only in himself, but in his park. There's a story I've read in many of the books about Walt's run-in with contradiction at Disneyland. He was walking through Tomorrowland when he saw a cast member from Frontierland, in full costume, strolling through. As a storyteller Walt was aghast. This one detail completely upended the story of Tomorrowland. A land of the future would not have cowboys!

As a result, the Disney Imagineers are meticulous about setting for their lands. They create a seamless package of details, some so small you probably never noticed, in order to immerse you in the experience. Costumes, sounds, fonts, plants and even pavement change as you go from land to land. Frontierland's pavement is pockmarked and stamped with horseshoe prints while Main Street, U.S.A. uses brick roadways. Tomorrowland is colored in futuristic metallic silvers while Adventureland is filled with natural browns and greens. The buildings in Fantasyland evoke a fairy tale version of medieval Europe with brick walls and tall spires while those in New Orleans Square are so true to life that my sister, who visited New Orleans, said of the visit, only half-jokingly, "don't bother, you've seen it already."

Then there are the surprising details that drive the setting home. The plants of Adventureland are large and natural in appearance while those of Tomorrowland are orderly, small, sustainable and edible. (My young cousin can attest that they do not all however taste good.) One can see even more subtle differences in plants in the planter between the entrances to Adventureland and Frontierland. Looking closely, one finds that the garden is split in half. The plants and flowers are not very different, but they are different. The Adventureland side is just a little wilder to imply its more natural setting. Adventureland also has the most winding paths and obstructed sight lines in the park, leaving you with a sense of wonder and adventure as you question what may be waiting just around the bend. It just wouldn't be the same if you were walking by the Jungle Cruise on a gray, concrete sidewalk with modern pop music playing in the background. Those contradictions would pull you out of the story. You might as well be at Six Flags!

Disneyland is not Six Flags. The identity of Disneyland is clear and Imagineers work hard to maintain it. Disneyland is a theme park, not an amusement park. The rides are themed carefully to fit their story. You won't just see "the world's tallest/fastest/etc. roller coaster!" style marketing at a Disney park. In the few cases where the Imagineers "missed" and created attractions that would be more at home in an amusement park like California Screamin' and the original Ferris Wheel at Disney California Adventure they eventually rethemed them to fit a story. California Screamin', a fairly standard roller coaster with a loop is now the Incredicoaster telling the story of trying to catch a runaway Jack-Jack. The Ferris Wheel is now the Pixar Pal Around, a stretch to reach a story to be sure, but an attempt nonetheless! That entire area of California Adventure, now known as Pixar Pier, but previously known as The Boardwalk, underwent a makeover in 2018 to make it fit the Disney identity.

In fact, nearly all of Disney California Adventure has undergone a makeover since its opening in 2001. When it opened, the park had a lot of California and very little Disney. It featured a small roller coaster themed after Mulholland Drive in San Francisco. There was a store called San Andreas Shakes. There was even an entire area dedicated to the thrilling topic of California agriculture. The idea was to provide a taste of all of California in one location for visiting tourists. This was flawed for many reasons. First, tourists didn't come to Disneyland to experience California. They came to California to experience Disneyland! Secondly, annual passholders, who are a very significant portion of visitors, already lived in California. We didn't need to see fake versions when the real thing was literally right outside the park. Lastly, it just didn't appeal to children. There were few, if any, Disney characters or references to be seen. Restaurants had adult-oriented themes like soap operas and served alcohol. To the Imagineers' credit they did follow Commandment 7 and were sure to tell just one story at a time, but, as we saw in the last chapter, the Disney story is creating joy for kids and adults together. Disney's California Adventure was clearly not first designed with this story in mind and it failed mightily as a result.

Today, only a few attractions remain in their original state (Grizzly River Run, Golden Zephyr and Jumpin' Jellyfish.) Disney-specific touches have been added throughout the park (such as retheming Mulholland Madness as Goofy's Sky School.) Many of the original California-specific attractions have disappeared. Cars Land and Pixar Pier have added many more kid-friendly options. The park still is clearly themed around California, but now also fits the Disney identity of a place both kids and adults can enjoy. In fact, it has reached the point now where Disney fans can have a debate on which park they prefer and not sound completely crazy if they choose Disney California Adventure (which I would!) If the Imagineers had avoided contradictions from the beginning, they would have avoided the frustration of having to spend over a billion dollars to redesign and save the park!

I too experienced the frustration of breaking this commandment in my classroom. It happened from the very beginning. Unfortunately, it took me years to realize it. I was hired for my position straight out of college. I had done a semester of student teaching, but most of my training had come through my college's teacher education program. That program was built largely around the ideas of Harry Wong. His *The First Days of School* was the text for more than one class. I remember reading it, and rereading it, the summer before I started. I had been sold a dream by my professors. If I just had strict procedures for everything in my classroom, I'd have the same smiling face as Mr. Wong. If I just created worksheets with very clear objectives, I'd have the most successful students I possibly could. I bought it completely. I came in out of the gates with a detailed syllabus, tons of procedures and lots of practice.

Almost none of it worked.

My students, to my utter shock, didn't always follow the procedures like they did in the videos we saw in college. They rarely bothered to read the objectives on the very detailed worksheets I created. They acted out, I gave them consequences, and nothing changed. I can still vividly remember that first year when I'd finally lost it and asked one of my students, Nick, with exasperation "What's with you?" I literally could not square his behavior with all I'd been taught. He just laughed and mockingly replied back to me "What's with *you*?!" I realized then I had lost. I wasn't happy. I wasn't me. Worst of all, the students knew it.

My second year was a fairly similar experience to the first. It was better since I didn't feel so buried in creating new plans all the time, but the behavior problems continued, and I really wasn't enjoying myself much at all. I read *The First Days of School* again. This time, I found myself asking "What's with me?" just like Nick had. I started, slowly, to realize that I wasn't being me. I was full of contradictions. I told my students I wanted them to feel safe and take risks in my class, then I'd slam them with an instant consequence when they took a risk I didn't like. I thought I had to. Harry Wong told me! The students realized I wasn't being authentic. Nick, and many others, didn't know how to react in my classroom because I wasn't giving them a consistent vision. I was making contradictions left and right. I was trying to be someone else.

When I started to be myself in my classroom everything changed. My students were happier and more engaged and so was I. When I realized I really didn't care if a student got up to sharpen a pencil without asking it took a ton of pressure off of me. I didn't have to constantly be thinking "if I let that go, I'll lose them forever." as I'd been taught. My list of rules got shorter and shorter every year. This meant that I could be extremely strict about those things which bothered me most. Eventually, as I noted previously, I stopped teaching rules entirely. Instead, on day one, I tell my students that I respect them and trust that they know how to be students. I add that one thing that really bothers me is when people are late. As long as they show up on time and act like students there won't be any issues. I don't believe people need to earn respect. Respect should be automatic to our fellow man. If I tell my students I respect them then immediately go into a lengthy, repetitive list of rules and consequences I'm undermining myself. I might as well be a cowboy walking through Tomorrowland! I'd much rather let them find the edges on their own.

Walt had a similar philosophy. Early in the park's life a cast member was concerned that guests might vandalize a beautiful new car built for Main Street, U.S.A. Walt said, "Don't worry about it. Just make them (the cars) beautiful and you'll appeal to the best side of people. They all have it. ... All you have to do is bring it out."

That is authentic to the teacher I want to be and it works. I have very few discipline problems in my classroom. My students are no different than those anywhere else. They have their days and they certainly misbehave from time to time. The difference in my classroom is that those behaviors are less frequent and, almost always, very quickly corrected. Often all I have to do is ask my students a simple question; "Whose class are you in right now?" That's usually all it takes to bring them back to where I want them. They just need that quick reminder of what I expect of them. Sometimes that won't be enough, and we'll need to talk outside for a minute. Again, I just ask questions. I start with "So, what is going on today?" They rarely answer. In truth, they often don't know. Their developing brains just can't keep up with everything that is going on! A few seconds of silent thought lets them calm down. I then remind them of whichever of my expectations on which they may have come up short. Sometimes they apologize, sometimes they just nod, but almost always that's enough. The problem is solved and doesn't repeat.

I fully realize this all sounds crazy. It likely seems that my students just walk all over me. I assure you, they don't. I am incredibly strict with my expectations. Few of my students see me as strict though. They instead understand that I am just being myself. Due to my frustration with people being late, I start at the bell, often before, because I have specific plans I want to complete. As such, one of my expectations is not only that students be in the room before the bell, but are both seated and working before the bell rings. Early in the year I get the "I was inside!!!" response when I give a tardy warning. I just ask that question, "Whose classroom are you in right now?" That ends it. After just a few days my class starts itself. They don't even need me to come in the room for the first five minutes. (Which is a great opportunity to greet them outside and chat with a few about their day to learn a little more about my audience!)

To have this work you must be consistent with the rules that do matter. If I assign a consequence for an action once, I had better do so the next time as well. If I don't, either things slip out of my control or kids see me as wildly unfair. (Harry Wong was right about some things!) Sometimes this isn't comfortable, but it has to be done. Years ago, I assigned a discipline essay to one of my favorite human beings, not just students, of all time for talking at the beginning of class. Vanessa had never been in trouble in her life. She was in my AVID class, played games in my room at lunch and talked with me all the time — a student that any teacher would want. I hated giving her the essay, but I had to. Everyone else was quiet. It would be a huge contradiction if I let it slide. Clearly, it made an impact. I never had another issue with her talking at the wrong time and she never let me forget about giving her that essay, even when I saw her again at high school graduation! Consistency works.

Think about how Disneyland handles rules and manages their guests. We've already established that they don't make you sign a rules list to enter the park. Yet, we know they do have rules in place. Disneyland cast members don't walk up to you when you enter a store and say, "If you steal anything in here you'll face consequences." That doesn't mean they are lax on their rules. It means they know that you know stealing is wrong. Yet, assuredly, if you violate their rules, even if they are unstated, you'll hear about it. That's not a contradiction, that's consistency. They want you to feel free to explore and enjoy yourself.

For us, guest management, or classroom management, is often defined by how one disciplines a class. I think instead it ought to be seen as how one leads a class. Discipline is obviously part of leading, but it certainly isn't the whole thing. This is why it is so important to be yourself in your classroom. If I try to lead my students somewhere I don't really care to go, it just isn't going to work. I have to know my primary goals and intentions (my story!) to lead properly.

Disney's leadership story is based on four principals in order of importance; safety, courtesy, show, and efficiency. Having these principals makes it easy to make decisions and lead.

Every decision is run through those four lenses. I once saw this played out firsthand while waiting in line for the Haunted Mansion attraction. The regular line was running about a 30-minute wait, on the high end for the attraction. I used a FastPass so my wait was only about 5 minutes before I reached the stretching room. When the room finished stretching, I exited out into a very crowded hallway. I managed to make a bit of progress before realizing we weren't moving at all. Then, the horrifying "We have been unavoidably detained by peckish (or is it puckish?) spirits, please remain seated in your *Doom Buggy*. Your tour will resume shortly." rang out. This same message would repeat roughly 5 times in the next 20 minutes as we remained, unmoving, in the tightly packed hallway.

Eventually, the lights in the hall came on and a cast member came out to explain that the attraction would resume shortly, but anyone who wanted to exit now could follow her. She also explained, in her frustration, that the ride had been stopped due to some riders behaving inappropriately. A few people followed her to the exit, but surprisingly few. The attraction restarted a few minutes later and all seemed right with the world.

Hundreds, at least, of guests' experiences were delayed and disrupted by only a couple of people misbehaving. Sure sounds like my classroom at times. In this case the guests were a bit annoyed, but not overly so. You'd expect a lot of anger and frustration in such a situation, but there was surprisingly little. Yes, people were annoyed — nobody likes to have their planned experiences disrupted —, but they mostly remained calm. I imagine the guests waiting in the outside line, those that couldn't hear the ride delay announcement, were frustrated, but when I exited the ride the line was still full. They hadn't quit and left either.

Why? Guests know the story. Disney's primary concern is safety because it is the guest's primary concern as well. It may not seem that way when you see people rampaging toward the next attraction with their heads buried in a cell phone screen but, for proof, look at the tremendous drop in Disney attendance in the years immediately after 9/11. If people don't feel safe, they aren't visiting the park. It is why guests are willing to wait in a 20-minute security check line after having just waited in a 20-minute tram line before they've even entered the park. In this case, Disney cast members were willing to risk the frustration of hundreds of guests by stopping the ride. They were not willing to risk their safety by letting it continue.

I later ran into who I have to assume were the misbehaving guests. While waiting in line for Astro Blasters a couple hours later I heard a man ask one of the cast members, "So, what are the rules for this ride?" The cast member clearly was confused. "What do you mean?" The guest replied, "Like, what should I not do?" They told me if I break another rule I'd get kicked out." So, not only did Disney's story of safety first keep their guests safe, it also seemed to alter the inappropriate behavior!

What is your story?

My first day of student teaching in 2002 I remember telling my students I wanted my class to be a balance of two conflicting terms: safety and risk. Students should be safe in their classrooms. Safe from physical threat, safe from ridicule and safe to be themselves. When they feel this way, hopefully, they will be willing to take risks, show vulnerability and grow. That has remained my classroom story to this day. As shown in the previous chapter, telling this story starts on day 1 and, in fact, minute 1 of my class.

The story plays out in far more than just words. Very early on in my classes I give students more freedom than they are accustomed to. As I mentioned, I don't go over rules with my students. I tell them "you know how to be students; I'll trust you to be students." That trust pays off. When the first one asks to use the pencil sharpener, I tell them "Of course, and you don't need to ask, just use it politely." Again, by and large, I have no issues with the sharpener becoming a disruption. Students politely get up, wait until I'm done talking, sharpen their pencil, and sit back down. If I am telling them with my words that my room is a safe place where they can trust taking risks, I have to show through my actions that I trust them as well.

However, one of the problems that arises over a year in a classroom is that students get "too" comfortable (like Vanessa!) Disneyland isn't immune to this problem. Annual Passholders have earned some derogatory nicknames over the years and, often, with good cause. In 2018 Disneyland social clubs made news when a lawsuit was filed against one of the groups. According to an article in the *Los Angeles Times*, these social clubs look like roving biker gangs. They wear the same torn, denim vests emblazoned with various patches. They claim to be Disneyland superfans. They are in the park all the time and, like most of your students, don't cause any problems. They do silly things like "attraction take-overs" where they attempt to get every seat on an attraction filled by one of their members. The lawsuit alleged that one group was harassing another, and Disneyland had been complicit by not stopping them. The article closes with one club member commenting she'd never risk bad behavior for fear of having her annual pass taken away.

While we want our classrooms to be fun and welcoming, we can't forget that safety comes first. That means discipline has to play a real role in our classrooms. One of the greatest benefits of having a magical classroom is that students want to be there and want to participate in the experiences you offer. Like the woman who feared losing her access to Disneyland my students rarely want to lose access to my classroom. Still, they are middle schoolers and discipline takes place. As I discussed with my Feudalism lab, I have, at times, taken away full activities from certain periods. Safety must come first. This happens most often in activities that require student freedom. Some students, and sometimes whole classes, prove they can't handle such things. While my other periods participate in the experience, they get an alternate, very safe, activity. Most of the time this only has to happen once. They hear from their friends in the other periods what they missed and the next time I have an issue a reminder of the consequences is often enough to quickly resolve it. I absolutely hate taking away an activity, but I know Disneyland hates shutting down an attraction for thirty minutes. Sometimes, you just have to.

Along the same lines, when I cannot trust a class to behave properly in groups, I don't let them work in groups. As a student, I rarely felt safe in groups since I wanted to get work done while my group members often wanted anything but. In my class I'm not willing to let one or two kids ruin an experience for their group mates. If it's only a handful I'll just pull them from the activity, but I've had classes where there

are so many where that just isn't feasible. I'd rather pull the
experience than have it be a bad one.

The new Millennium Falcon: Smuggler's Run attraction
at Disneyland is a good example of how an experience can go
wrong when group members don't participate. The attraction
has six jobs filled by the riders: two pilots, two gunners and two
engineers. All three roles are needed to score well on the ride.
The better you do, the longer, and smoother, your experience.
On one of my rides I was in the engineer position along with
two pilots who did not even try to listen to the instructions on
how to fly the ship. Mind you, instructions are printed on your
personal role card and are given twice verbally — once by a live
cast member and once by a video. They didn't seem to care. As
a result, that particular experience was awful. Our ship kept
bouncing off of walls and, as a result, was shaking and jerking
rather violently. As our ship engineer I was so busy pushing
buttons and flipping switches for repairs that I had no time
to see where we were actually flying which led to significant
motion sickness. I've ridden the attraction multiple times and
every other experience was stellar. I've had 7-year-old pilots
who did just fine because they listened and worked with the
team. I had a pre-teen girl who flew and captained our ship like
a professional. She even gave us all a pep talk before we took off!
Collaborative experiences can be magical when everyone is on
board, but we have to be willing to close it off when they aren't.

To help students understand my expectations for group
work, very early in the year I do an activity adapted from *Teach
Like a PIRATE*. The story of the activity is that a plane has
crashed on a deserted island. A ship passes by that can carry
half, but only half, of the survivors back to safety. Students
collaborate to decide which ones to send home and which
to leave on the island. I personalize it by making one of the
characters a parody of me. I don't tell them I've done it, but a
few kids always pick up on it, even early in the year, and the
news spreads around the room. They get so into arguing who
to save that I have to cut off their debates after 20 minutes
or we'd take days to make a decision. It's fun, it's exciting, it
requires teamwork, the stakes feel high, but they can't really
fail — sounds like a perfect first collaborative activity to me!

Just like Hondo does before you board your ship in Smuggler's Run, I very explicitly lay out my group work expectations before the activity begins. I use a concept they are all familiar with from the video game world — team killers. These are players who, instead of seeking to win, just want to annoy people by shooting their own teammates. I always get a few students who excitedly blurt out "I do that!" Well, thank you for pointing out who to keep an eye on during the activity. Most kids though get the idea and admit how annoyed they get when people like that are on their team. It's a great set up and it means all I have to do when a student starts to go off task during group work is remind them we don't allow team killers in our class.

This is only one example of how we lead our classrooms. It isn't easy, and sometimes isn't fun, but we must be leaders in our classrooms. When we are, management comes more easily, and discipline is both less frequent and more effective. Be yourself and model what you want from your students. Don't be afraid to smile, laugh and joke if that's who you are. Maintain your identity and avoid contradictions! Sadly, leading, like presenting and planning, isn't taught very well in most teacher education programs. It comes naturally to some people, but I do believe it is also something that can be learned. Dozens of books have been written on how to be a leader. The previously mentioned *Creating Magic* by Lee Cockerell is one of my favorites. In it he boils down great leadership to its core characteristic saying, "Passion may contribute more to the greatness of a leader than any other trait. It is the driving force that enables people to attain far more than they ever imagined." You may not think you are a leader, but you certainly are passionate. I mean, you've made it this far!

So, find what you are passionate about and let it drive you! For me that means encouraging my students to push themselves to new levels and experiences. That's what ultimately led me to one of my most successful experiments, Choose Your Own Adventure, or CYOA. When I was a student in 8th grade, my history class operated much differently than my others. At the end of each unit we made newspapers with multiple articles, cartoons and puzzles. I found that I loved writing the articles, but had zero interest in any of the more artistic aspects of the project. My first few years as a teacher I tried bringing projects like this into my class, but kept running into the issue that I couldn't ever find a project that appealed to all of my students. Some loved the art projects while others hated them. Some loved writing creative stories with historical characters while others preferred simply answering questions out of a textbook. I wanted them to explore the more outside-the-box activities and find the joy in them that I did as a student.

I decided to provide some options for students. I started with just a handful. Students could create travel brochures, write a creative story, put on a play, design a board game or, create flashcards for the unit. I put the instruction sheets out in folders on the counter and told my students they were free to choose whatever option they felt fit them best. All the options were worth equal point values, so it really was up to them to pick. If we are constantly telling students to be themselves and find their passions, we need to give them opportunities to do so. If a student chose to do flashcards so be it! It's the last thing I would choose myself, but that was the point.

This system worked so well that I immediately thought about how to expand it. I wanted more options, clearer instructions and a uniform rubric for grading. Making grading as simple as possible is a huge part of maintaining my identity. I hate grading! I started designing instruction sheets for every type of output I could think of. I ended up with magazine covers, pop up displays, timelines, maps, wanted posters, poems, TV networks, iPhones, diary entries and a whole bunch more. I now have over 75 options from which students may choose. As I created new activities, I realized some clearly took more time and effort than others so I broke them up into different tiers based on how long they would take to finish. Then, I made a rubric that broke each activity down into just three components (avoiding overload!)- Effort, Evidence and Eccentricity. What I wanted most out of this process was to see students doing their best, providing accurate historical information and being creative. So, it didn't matter if I was grading trading cards or a remixed song, I was looking for the same basic things and my very simple rubric could apply.

However, one problem I ran into as I added more and more options was decision paralysis. At some point, and I don't know exactly when, there were just too many options for many students. There were so many things they wanted to try that they couldn't decide! I'd see students spend a full 45-minute period just looking over their options. To help stop that, I put artificial limits like saying they could only choose from the top row of activities (I had them in rows of folders on my wall at the time) or from a pre-selected list that I made before the project (which are now often called learning menus.) That helped, but it also just left kids wanting to do the ones that were locked, thinking they were somehow better than the options left open! That certainly wasn't my intent.

So, I broke the activities down into more logical categories. I started by splitting them by the type of work students would be doing. There are detective assignments that focus on facts and historical reasoning, art assignments that involve either drawing or creating projects and profiler assignments that involve getting inside a historical figure's head. (Originally, I called this psychologist, but found quickly that term had a negative connotation with some of my students.)

From there, students choose the point value they want to go after. Lower point activities are not necessarily easier; they just take less time and typically have more simple directions. I "lock" the highest point activities, which can take multiple hours to complete, behind achievement levels. Only students with an 80% or higher in the class can choose these activities. My lower achieving students, who tend to need the most direct guidance, don't have to worry about choosing from quite so many options or taking on tasks that may prove too complex. Since all students can choose from the lower point activities there is no stigma attached to doing them. No one ever looked down on me for choosing to go on so-called "kiddie rides" like Gadget's Go Coaster! The lower point activities aren't a punishment and most of my more challenged students appreciate the limit on their options as it helps them to focus on what they do choose to do. All students complete the same amount of total points in their packet regardless of their achievement levels.

This reorganization helped students quickly eliminate entire banks of choices. These adjustments have made it so most of my students are able to make decisions on which assignment to do and get started quickly. In the few cases where kids still can't decide, I step in and decide for them.

Disneyland uses similar techniques to help guide the myriad choices available in the park. There are dozens of attractions, shows and shops to choose from when you enter the park. While you are not given an itinerary, you do have a map outlining your options. To help you make your way through the park, the number of decisions at any one time are kept purposefully low. Most pathways will only go in one of two directions. Even the area with the most choice available – the park's central hub — limits you to heading towards one of four lands. Once you've made your way and entered the land then you have the next layer of choices open to you. Now you are picking from a much smaller list of attractions, shows and shops. Further, Imagineers can use their design tricks (use a wienie!) to guide you to specific attractions once you are on that closed path. Obviously, you have plenty of choices to make in Disneyland, but by limiting those choices at any given time they are easily made.

The guiding limits I put in helped the whole process work for more students and allowed CYOA to become a regular part of my classroom routine. The work my students do for Choose Your Own Adventure continues to impress me. When given the freedom to choose their output, some kids really shine. As a bonus, they get to maintain their identity as well! Additionally, these activities serve as great learning assessments — far better than a typical multiple-choice test. Instead of quizzing students on their trivia knowledge I'm now evaluating their ability to use what they've learned to create something new. Create is significantly higher on Bloom's taxonomy than recall! So, my kids are doing more and thinking more, but it doesn't feel like more work. These projects are consistent with my classroom philosophy and thus just seem to flow along with everything else.

Interestingly, however, my colleague next door who helped me design many of the activities used within CYOA tried the process for a couple years and didn't like it. He found his students were constantly bombarding him with questions. Mine did the same, but it is well within my personality to ignore them! He likes a bit more order in his classroom. I like a little energy (though some might call it chaos) in my classroom. I like kids to stretch what they think they can do in strange ways. I fully realize that isn't true of everyone. CYOA works for me because of who I am as a teacher — not because it is a magic pill that will work for everyone. Avoid contradictions!

Makin' Memories

Commandment 8: Avoid Contradictions, Maintain Identity

Make sure you don't say one thing and do (or imply) another. Figure out your personal goals and limits and make sure everything in your class fits within them.

* * *

Remember Me

Don't forget to be yourself! Take advice from others, but make sure it fits with who you are and what you want from your classroom.

*What parts of your non-school life can
you bring into your school life?*

When We're Human

When we're human and treat our students the same way discipline becomes both more effective and less necessary. Remind your students you care about them and then push them farther than they think they can go!

*What situations in your class can you plan to
handle with care and empathy and which ones
must be handled with consequences?*

Happy Working Song

When you give students choice in their work they will perform far better than when you assign the same project to everyone. Let your students maintain their identity as artists or writers and they'll be happy. When they are you will be too!

For your next assignment what is one alternate option you could offer your students?

* * *

One Little Spark
"Eliminating the things that contradict what we are seeing and saying makes our guests feel at home."
—Marty Sklar

There's a Great Big Beautiful Tomorrow
What's that thing you've been doing because someone told you to once, but it never felt right? Don't do it tomorrow. See what happens!

CHAPTER NINE

For Every Ounce of Treatment, Add a Ton of Treat

"In our business, Walt Disney said, you can educate people —, but don't tell them you're doing it! Make it fun!"

—Marty Sklar, *Dream It! Do It!*

The guests streamed in, slowly filling the seats in the massive warehouse that doubled for the set of *Who Wants to be a Millionaire?*

I picked up the remote tethered to the seatback in front of me. My fingers hovered over the buttons, prepared to press them at any hint of a question. I'd played Who Wants to be A Millionaire? Play It! enough times to know that just smashing 4 letters as quickly as possible was a viable strategy to winning a coveted spot in the hot seat. I'd also learned though that I could drastically increase my chances if I at least got the first answer of the Fastest Finger Question correct before randomly pushing the remaining three. In a room of 500ish people a few were going to get the sequence right just on sheer randomness. I had to be faster than random, but still give myself an edge by being more correct than just random guessing.

The producer gave instructions to the crowd, just like one would in a real TV taping. The guests practiced cheering for the soon-to-be-revealed host — it has to look good on camera! The music swelled, the suited host, doing his best Regis Philbin impersonation, walked in and the crowd exploded in cheers. Not me. My hands remained locked on that remote. I had a game to win.

I knew that any second the Fastest Finger Question would appear on the big screen. The host would read it aloud and guests would naively wait for him to finish and then put in their answer. The trick was to read faster than the host. Playing the game multiple times a day for months had surely paid off!

The host took his seat, the lights came down and the question came up. My fingers flew over the 4 buttons, finishing my inputs before the host finished reading the question. Moments later the crowd camera zoomed in on my face as I was revealed as the next contestant to take the hot seat. For the next 15 minutes I'd be answering very boring trivia questions in front of a cheering crowd enveloped by dramatic lighting and sound effects.

I reached the 500,000-point question, just one away from winning a Disney Cruise. I was out of Lifelines and all on my own. The energy was palpable. The crowd was fully behind me. The question was something about Scandinavian countries and population. Uh. No chance here. I took a shot with a semi-educated guess. The energy left the room immediately. Not-quite-Regis gave his consoling "oooh, sorry, no." My adventure was over.

The game itself, as with the real show and most trivia games, was pure treatment. Every now and then they'd throw in a Disney related question but, for the most part, they were just random trivia. There were questions ranging from Shakespeare to math and everything in between. The competition aspect of it made it a ton of fun, but so did the drama of cheering along with those in the "hot seat." 500 plus guests had just spent 20ish minutes receiving wildly uninteresting facts and knowledge. Yet, they loved every minute of it. There can be great joy in learning — even the boring stuff!

* * *

"I'm Not an Entertainer! (But I Should Be...)"

That was the title of my first keynote presentation given at a local education conference in 2011. Well before I realized that Disney Imagineers held all the secrets to designing the ideal classroom, I lobbied, from my own experience, for constantly adding fun to the classroom. Whether it was silly clips from *The Simpsons* or playing early PowerPoint review games like *Jeopardy* and *Who Wants to be a Millionaire*, I injected fun wherever I could. I knew that entertainment was the key to engagement. As I put it in that early presentation, an engaged audience is a learning audience!

We've likely all lamented "I'm not an entertainer!" at one time or another, myself included, but that usually comes when I'm trying to engage my students and failing miserably. I think that frustration is okay! Problems drive solutions. However, I've also heard some teachers say things like, "I'm not going to demean myself jumping on desks like Robin Williams in *Dead Poet's Society!*" I'm not saying you should (though I might if I thought I couldn't engage my students in any other way), but your audience's reactions should be a big part of your focus in any presentation — even in a classroom where they "have" to listen anyway. The fact is a big part of our job is presenting. As I've said, the techniques to do so well aren't really taught, and certainly aren't emphasized in teacher preparation programs, but it is one of the pillars of the profession. We have to be able to present in a fun way to engage our audience. Yes, we need to entertain them!

The Disney Imagineers mixed learning with entertainment from the very early days. Great Moments with Mr. Lincoln, for example, is a heavy dose of treatment. The show debuted at the New York World's Fair in 1964. A plaque on the wall outside the attraction, which now sits in the Disneyland Opera House, tells us that Abraham Lincoln was Walt Disney's hero growing up. So much so that he would go to school dressed as Lincoln and recite his speeches. Though the show has gone through many modifications over the decades it has always been a story of Lincoln's rise to prominence and featured a recitation of a segment of the *Gettysburg Address*. It has had many types of "fun" included over those revisions from booming lights as cannons blew (which is where I drew the inspiration for a similar effect in my Vicksburg Siege lesson mentioned in Chapter 4) to a chill-inducing haircut sequence using extremely clear stereo audio. What's most notable though is that the attraction features, what was at the time of its creation, one of the most advanced animatronic figures in the world. At the end of the show a curtain rises showing a seated Lincoln preparing to speak directly to the audience. The subtle head movements and shifting of his eyes are impressive and incredibly lifelike. Audiences at the World's Fair were so convinced he was real that they'd throw pennies at it to see if it would react like a human would! The real treat comes with the swelling of the music as Lincoln stands up to deliver the speech. It is a powerful "wow" moment as the statuesque figure rises like a real human. Other animatronic figures in the park move but, until the recent additions of Rocket Raccoon in Guardians of the Galaxy Mission Breakout and Hondo Ohnaka in Millennium Falcon Smuggler's Run, none in such a dramatic, lifelike way.

Disney's use of fun in support of treatment has only grown since the creation of Mr. Lincoln. In 2012 Disney California Adventure started hosting a Lunar New Year celebration. It had been hosted at Disneyland park for a while previously, but wasn't a particularly big deal. It often lasted only a day or two and was little more than a parade. I didn't even know it existed until I showed up to the park in 2018 and experienced the festivities myself. I didn't expect much. In fact, I almost didn't even bother to check it out. From what I could tell from the map, it was tucked away in the corner of the park and didn't seem like it would have much to offer.

I'm glad the world history teacher inside of me pushed me to check it out because my first impression was way off. It was a big deal with tons to offer! That entire corner area of the park was decked out in traditional Asian stylings and decorations. Asian musical artists performed traditional and contemporary Asian songs on the stages throughout the area. It was definitely a ton of fun, but I also felt like I got a great taste of Asian culture.

Apparently, I wasn't the only one who was impressed as the 2019 version was an even grander experience. The event grew in size, expanding quite a bit out of its corner. It now had its own dedicated store (with a super cool door hanger that I will forever regret not buying immediately because it was gone the next time I passed by!) and the small parade, which they called a processional, starring Mulan and Mushu grew to a huge event. Asian instrumental music with a modern flair played through the area and beyond. Taiko drummers performed multiple shows a day. Food menus were changed to include Asian fare from different countries like Vietnam and Korea.

As a teacher what I really loved was the amount of cultural and historical content provided. There were information displays throughout the festival with background information on the various Asian countries which were represented. There was another with information about the different Chinese birth animals. The treatment was so well mixed in with the fun that it didn't feel like treatment at all.

The Imagineers used similar tactics in the 2019 Plaza De Familia event also at California Adventure. This was an event based around the film *Coco* and was a celebration of the Dia De Los Muertos holiday. The festival had multiple cultural events ranging from Mariachi performers to writing down a memory of a loved one to hang on a tree. All of this was couched in fun. A puppet version of *Coco*'s Miguel danced and sang his way through the plaza. Kids colored traditional Day of the Dead masks and had their faces painted. Like with the Lunar New Year celebration, Disney took the opportunity to add some treatment as well. At the entrance to the plaza stood two large sign boards with information about the traditions represented in the festival. The signs themselves were pure treatment. They were literally just large blocks of text (of course with a small touch of visual literacy with a unique font), but by placing them amongst the fun they became part of it and were thus far more engaging.

Disney clearly understands the need to include fun with education so when they designed a new training program for employees, particularly with the goal of improving employee retention, they made sure plenty of fun was present. They found that Disney employees quickly became jaded when the story of Disney magic and joy sold to them in training didn't match up with their hard, physical work experience (they didn't avoid contradictions!) This training arm of Disney became known as Disney University. It has been used to train Disney cast members all around the world in Disney parks and Disney stores. The training is a heavy dose of treatment including things like company safety policies, dress codes and contract issues. Much of it is typical training and HR stuff, but it sure isn't delivered in a typical way. It is hands-on, experiential, and yes, fun. Doug Lipp in *Disney U* describes it this way: "Every training event is an opportunity to be creative and interesting rather than the opposite: dull and academic." Can we say the same about our lessons?

Of course, we'd love to be able to just focus on fun all the time. However, we, admittedly, have a different main goal in mind than Disney (but not really *that* different from Disney University, we want to keep our students from checking out too.) Whereas education is a nice byproduct of the entertainment they provide, for us it has to be the focus. That doesn't mean that fun can't play a huge role or even be the central organizing feature of our classrooms. It can and it should.

Let's start with the simplest way to add fun to an experience, humor. I discussed the Jungle Cruise a few times already. As a ride it is pretty darn boring. The animatronics are very primitive. In many cases the animals don't move at all. The boats are slow and feature cramped and uncomfortable seats. Yet, it is an attraction I rarely miss on my frequent visits to Disneyland. The ride itself, however, is not the reason why. It is the humor built into it that makes it fun and into a complete attraction.

Yet, when it first opened, the attraction was nearly all treatment. The narration sounded much like one of *Walt Disney's True Life Adventure* nature documentaries on which the ride was based. Within a few years the attraction grew stale. It just wasn't fun more than once. So, Disney Imagineer Marc Davis was given the task of reimagining the attraction. He remade it into a series of comical vignettes such as the scene where a bunch of explorers are climbing a pole to avoid an angry rhinoceros. Jokes were injected into the skipper script and have been updated and added to constantly since. The attraction is filled with jokes from beginning to end. It is now 10 minutes of pure fun — as long as you can appreciate puns! Some of the jokes have become classics that are told nearly every time through (such as "the 8th wonder of the world — the backside of water! O2H! O2H!") whereas others have been a result of ad-libbing and quickly disappeared (such as my personal favorite that I only ever heard once, "We have to make a sharp turn, lean to the right, lean to the right! Don't worry, it's okay, we're in Orange County!") The Jungle Cruise is the one attraction at Disneyland that you can truly say is never the same twice.

When we inject humor into our classrooms, we add that dose of fun that truly makes the treatment go down easily. Plus, as we discussed in Chapter 8, when it is consistent with who we are, it has the added benefit of making us more human and relatable. We can do it through our usual day to day interactions with our students or by designing it into our lessons. Just be yourself and be open to having a good time. One of my favorite tricks is to take historical images and turn them into jokes. It can be as simple as making Andrew Jackson's portrait frown when he hears the results of the election of 1824 or as complex as making Queen Elizabeth's portrait wink and make kissing motions when she "hears" me talk about Walter Raleigh and Francis Drake. Both animations can be done with several computer programs, but the one I prefer is *CrazyTalk*. With it you can bring life to any static image. I've also used it to have historical portraits "talk" to students and even to make the Mona Lisa start moving subtly as we discuss how she looks so realistic that she might come to life at any moment. I add humor to that experience by pretending I don't see the movement. I play dumb when my students inevitably say, "I think she just moved!" by saying "yes, that's how skilled Da Vinci was!"

It's a lot of fun to take absurd situations like this in your content area and play them out as if they were really happening. One I like to do each year comes up when teaching about the Magna Carta, probably one of the least humorous documents ever written. As we review the different clauses, which outline such hilarious situations as church — state relations and the trial rights of nobles, we come upon one which simply states that the king cannot force a person to build bridges at river crossings. I pause and stare at it silently for a second. Then, I say "You know, I don't know how they came up with this list, but I can only imagine how that one ended up on it." I then weave a story about a brainstorming session where they come up with these great ideas for human rights, but there's one guy in the back who has terrible ideas every time. One says "hey, let's ask for fair taxes!," another "let's demand we can't be forced to go off to war!," then from the back he pipes in with "Yeah and uh... uh... he... uh... can't make us build bridges!" They reject him over and over, but he just keeps mentioning the bridge until they finally give up and put it on the list. The kids love the story and you can guess which of the clauses they never forget!

I know what some of you are thinking. "Mr. Roughton, I'm not funny. I told you I'm not even an entertainer and now you want me to be a stand-up comic?!" First of all, of course you're funny. There isn't a funny gene that some are born with. Being funny comes from knowing your audience. You subvert their expectations and they laugh. There, I've revealed comedy's deepest secret. Luckily for us we have an easily amused audience. You do not need a deeply layered joke with a complex set up. Just watch any of the YouTube personalities kids enjoy. Most of them just yell and scream at random moments, subverting expectations, and that's enough for most teens to laugh. Surely you can do better than that! They are expecting you to be prim and proper all the time. Drop in random slang now and then and watch them lose it. Stare at them when they do something silly then slowly walk away without saying a word. They'll bust up! We have a pretty unique audience situation where they are all pretty much all the same age and mental state. Figure out a few good jokes and use them over and over. We've only got to hit one target.

Think about what a Jungle Cruise Skipper must contend with! Not only do they have to appeal to all ages, but they have people from hundreds of different cultural backgrounds and life situations. Puns using double-meaning English words don't work particularly well with people who don't speak English! I read a story in *Skipper Stories: True Tales from Disneyland's Jungle Cruise* where a skipper explained that when he has a guest with a hearing impairment that uses a signer his puns make no sense because they are translated literally. "It looks like they couldn't get the car to turn over!" becomes "It looks like they couldn't get the car upside-down!" While not every student will get our jokes every time at least we don't have quite that level of challenge!

If you're still not convinced you can be funny don't be discouraged. There are plenty of other ways to bring fun into your classroom. One that anyone can do is wear a costume. Disneyland was designed as a place for people to live out the

movies they saw on the big screen. Part of that was including the characters from those movies. Of course, including a
two-dimensional, animated mouse would require some pretty
fancy technology. Disney did the next best thing. They made
costumes! Even today in our advanced modern world where
kids have the technology to see and do almost anything literally in the palms of their hands they still line up and wait to
meet someone dressed as a giant mouse!

On one trip to Disneyland I was way in the back of the park
near the entrance to Mickey's Toontown. There's a popcorn
kiosk there and not a whole lot else and my mom had to buy the
newest collectible popcorn holder. There is also, however, apparently a door that leads to the backstage area. You can't even see
it until you are walking away from Toontown as it is tucked into
a corner. I only noticed it this time because there was a crowd
of guests lined up there. Being curious (and working on a book
about Disney!) I had to see what the excitement was.

At the front of the line stood a young woman with long,
red, curly hair wearing a blue-green, medieval style dress. It
was Merida from the movie *Brave*. Well, technically it was a
cast member wearing a costume and a wig made to look like
Merida from *Brave*, but you wouldn't have known that from
the people meeting her. And surely, it was *people* meeting her,
not just kids. There were plenty of twenty-somethings waiting
in line to take their picture with her as well. After about
twenty minutes the line had not dwindled in the slightest.
Merida announced in her Scottish accent that she had received
a message that a few of her brothers were in trouble and she
had to go help them. She scurried behind the "Cast Members
Only" door, much to the disappointment of those still waiting
in line. All for a young woman in a costume!

On any given trip you can see this happening all over both
parks. Some characters are so popular that they have been
given their own personal meeting areas. Mickey is always in
his house in Toontown, along with a "Your wait to meet Mickey
is X minutes" sign at the entrance. Anna and Elsa are available
nearly all day long in their version of Arendelle inside of the
Animation building in California Adventure. Tinkerbell and
her friends await in Pixie Hollow and a menagerie of princesses

can be found in the Fantasy Faire. Do not underestimate the power of a costume!

My classroom costumes tend to be historical outfits to match the time period. I don't wear many so when I do it makes quite an impact. I've dressed as a Roman senator for our Julius Caesar investigation, a monk for our Crusades experience, George Washington (complete with ridiculous wig) for our Constitutional Convention simulation and even, as I mentioned, a plague doctor with a creepy bird mask for our Black Death mystery. None of them were particularly expensive. Most were purchased during after Halloween sales at a deep discount. It certainly takes effort to put them together and wear them all day, but the gain in fun is well worth it.

Seeing the students' reaction when I open the door and greet them in full costume is a delight. Even the most jaded teenager laughs. Even better, wearing a costume really helps them drop their guard and play along with the activity. In the Crusade activity we travel around the school on our journey completing tasks along the way. Students bring a sword (their pencil), shield (notebook) and map (worksheet) with them. They are told to defend me, the monk, from any barbarians (students from other classes) along the way. Kids who are usually way too cool to act like kids hold up their pencils and binders and form a circle around me when approached and I don't even have to ask. The costume is fun, and it gives them permission to be silly and have fun too. The adults at Disneyland know that the young woman isn't Merida, but who cares? She plays it real, so they feel they have permission to do so as well. When we wear a costume, it does the same. We're willing to be vulnerable and silly, so our students join in.

Sometimes you don't even need a full costume — just a hat will do! My FeudalSIM activity I discussed in chapter 6 involves students and myself playing the roles of various players in a feudal kingdom. From the beginning when I started doing this lab over a decade ago I had a cheap, plastic crown that the student playing the monarch wore during the activity. In the days and weeks following, the students would rush to get to class just to wear the crown for a few minutes. It was silly, but it was fun. Years later I came across a ridiculous wool knit cap that was made to look like a Viking helmet complete with wool horns. What really put it over the top was the inclusion of a yarn beard with braids sewn into the bottom of the cap. I started putting it on just before I attacked the castles in the simulation. The roars of laughter when I popped up from under my desk in this ridiculous costume were deafening. A few years ago, I added one more hat. For most of the simulation I play the role of Pope, so I bought an oversized miter to wear. I didn't need a full costume. Just greeting them at the door with that giant thing on my head was plenty to bring in the fun.

You can also use physical props that you don't have to wear. With the Crusades activity, in addition to wearing the costume, I have an oversized scroll that I unfurl when I'm reading the pope's speech. It always gets a good laugh. As I read through it I pause at various points and hold up a shoddily made "Applause" sign. It is literally a ruler with a piece of paper with "APPLAUSE!" written on it taped to it. Laughter explodes throughout the room (along with hearty applause!) without fail. When a student is too cool to join in, I make a point to walk over to them and hold the sign right up to them and clear my throat with a powerful "ahem!" This will usually cause them to drop their defenses and join in. If nothing else, it makes them laugh! I will also, at one point, put the sign immediately back up after putting it down to restart the applause break. Once again, they laugh hard. Comedy is all about subverting expectations!

Unfortunately, I've often heard my colleagues lament "It's so easy to do stuff like that in social studies!" I won't deny that. Yes, it helps that I teach a subject that is built around people, objects and stories. That does not mean that you can't use costumes and props in other subjects. I've seen science teachers dressed as Sherlock Holmes for investigative labs. I've seen English teachers dressed as the Cat in the Hat. I've even seen math teachers dressed as dice! The goal of wearing a costume is to add fun. It doesn't have to be a museum-quality representation. I have no clue if the miter I wear as pope is correct for the time period. It almost certainly isn't. No student has ever cared! They see it, they laugh, they have fun. That's what we're going for and teachers of any subject can do that. These props and costumes make for an unforgettable learning experience. What props and costumes, even poorly created ones, could you use to bring magic to your classroom?

Another way to bring in fun to any subject is with games. Disney has jumped onto this layer of fun fairly recently with the creation of the *Play Disney Parks* app. The idea behind the app is to give guests fun things to do, primarily simple games, while waiting in line for attractions (which certainly counts as treatment). The games were mostly designed for those attractions whose lines are the longest such as Peter Pan's Flight and Space Mountain. Many are just basic trivia games centered around whichever land you happen to be in at the time or simple tap-the-right-thing-at-the-right-time kind of games. Still, I play them all the time when I'm in line.

However, as with many things in Galaxy's Edge, the Disney Imagineers really upped the ante with the game in the new land. The game is called *Star Wars: Data Pad*. It is a much deeper experience that plays directly with the land. With it you can scan shipping crates, listen to radio chatter and hack everything from door panels to huge fighter ships. Again, none of the activities are particularly interesting or deep on their own, but all the while you are completing quests, unlocking new outfits, and earning points for your chosen faction. The game feeds into the overall narrative that you are part of the story of the land. I get so immersed that it is no surprise I didn't hear those two stormtroopers coming up behind me!

Games have been used to teach for as long as there has been something worth teaching. It was Albert Einstein who said, "Play is the highest form of research." Even animals in the wild frequently learn through play as any tiger cub pouncing on its mother will prove. (That must be true, I saw it in the *Lion King*.) We seem to do a great job with this at lower grades, though even there play has largely been squeezed out, but as our students get older we do less and less of it. That is a huge mistake. We need more games!

Content review games based on game shows are a great first step to using games in your classroom. Along with the previously mentioned *Who Wants to be a Millionaire* and *Jeopardy*, I've made games based on *Deal or No Deal?* and *Figure it Out* for my students. I've also seen templates built around *Wheel of Fortune*, *$100,000 Pyramid* and *Family Feud*. They make for a great review before a test or quiz. Of these, *Jeopardy* seems to be the most popular among teachers with multiple websites dedicated to providing ways to make your own game. You input your own answers and questions and the game generates a *Jeopardy* board. I usually split my students into groups when we play as a class. I make it a bit of a race as the first group where all members have the answer, er... question, written down correctly and held in the air earns double points. All groups still have a chance to answer and earn the stated point value. This ensures that everyone is involved in every question. We don't want the fun to overshadow the treatment!

The other games are just small variations on this idea. For *Who Wants to Be a Millionaire?* I have one student sit in the hot seat at the front of the class. When he or she answers three questions in a row correctly or misses a question then someone in the audience with the correct answer takes the seat. In their time in the seat that may use any one of the Lifelines. The point values and reaching the million-dollar question doesn't matter for the rewards, but the kids still feel the drama and get excited as we make our way through what is essentially just a list of 15 fairly boring, content-based, trivia questions. With *Deal or No Deal?* the whole class plays as a team and as students answer questions, they also choose a case which is eliminated. The "banker" calls now and then (a great opportunity for humor!) to make offers and the class votes to take it or play on. Middle schoolers always play on! The points earned go into the class point bank for the inter-class competition that is always running in my classroom.

There are also web-based games like *Kahoot* and *Gimkit* that are designed for classrooms. These work similarly, but have the extra fun touch of using technology. In these games students submit their answers through a web-enabled device such as a cellphone or Chromebook. The game technology manages keeping score and leaderboards. While they may not have the TV game show themes, they are still a ton of fun!

Much like Disney has done with the *Play Disney Parks* app I've embedded these and other games into my overall class game layer. In Chapter 3 I outlined how my class is organized around the story of the Fracture Crisis. At the highest level it is a simple classroom management game. I keep a scoreboard up where classes earn and lose points depending on behavior. When a class reaches a predetermined point threshold, they win a class reward and the points start over. It is simple, so simple that I can barely classify it as a game. However, it is a start and students have fun with it. At the very least it helps with classroom management.

To make it more of a game I added a component called "The Bonus Round." On Fridays each class plays a mini game where they can spend the points they've earned that week to earn more points or "attack" other classes. I have one version like *Let's Make a Deal* where they can pay to open doors and get whatever waits behind them and another that works like a roulette wheel where they pay points to buy spins. I made both games in PowerPoint and themed them around my other pop culture love — video games. The doors open up to prizes like "1 UP — Gain 100 points" or "Tetris! Equalize your points with another squad." The games are ridiculously simple and take no more than 5 minutes to play, yet the students absolutely love them. They beg to be the leader each week and are extremely quick to remind me if I forget to play the game with them. It's a sign of how starved for fun our kids are that such a simple game can bring about such excitement!

There must be more to why basic games like this are so successful. It's simple really — competition is fun! I talked about the two *Toy Story* themed attractions in Chapter 3. Both are fairly simple as far as attractions go. You sit in a car and follow a track. It is the competitive aspect that makes them so fun and ensures that each ride feels different from the rest. Each time I ride I try different strategies. I aim for different targets, try to activate different bonuses and try to figure out how I can best work with the others in my car to earn the highest scores. At the end of each ride your score is displayed and you're given a rank, which means nothing. Still, I'm always pushing to reach the next level!

The Imagineers have also used competition elements in two of their most recent "E-ticket" attractions — Radiator Springs Racers and Smuggler's Run. In Racers the competition is a key part of the story since you are living out the movie *Cars*. After passing through the dark ride portion of the attraction two of the ride vehicles line up next to each other for a race. You get an energetic 3 — 2 — 1 countdown and the cars zoom forward together. As they continue around banked turns and over stomach-dropping hills, the cars pull in front of one another multiple times before a last second photo finish ends the race.

On the other hand, in Smuggler's Run there is no direct competitor. Much like in the two *Toy Story* attractions, you earn points as you complete various tasks on the ship. While you do get to see your individual score, it is the combined score of your crew that is displayed at the end and, if you're playing along, saved to your *Star Wars Data Pad* character. The score tracking adds competition and that fun little challenge of trying to do a little better each time you ride. You also get the added bonus of the attraction lasting longer the better you do. There's nothing wrong with holding activities back until students hit a certain achievement level!

What's notable about both of these attractions is that the competition isn't real, or at least, isn't what we traditionally think of as real competition. In the case of Racers, you have no agency over the outcome of the race. You win or lose based on a computer's decision. In Smuggler's Run you are competing strictly against yourself. You get a score at the end, but it isn't compared to anyone else's. There are no leaderboards or "You Win!" screens like there are in the *Toy Story* attractions. Apparently, just the illusion of competition is enough to add fun to an experience!

There is also a not-really-competitive individual reward layer to the Fracture Crisis. As students complete activities (known as missions) in class they earn experience points (XP). They can also earn XP by completing optional side quests such as playing a content-based game or researching a specific topic. The only competition here is that the top XP earner every grading period gets their picture posted to the Wall of Champions, so they are immortalized in my classroom. The main focus are the power ups they can earn as they work to raise their personal scores. As they gain XP they level up. At each of the 10 levels they earn new rewards ranging from small ones like a piece of candy at level 1 to lunch on me at level 10. There are more practical rewards like the ability to work with a partner on any assignment or requiring me to make a positive phone call home. The opportunity to level up makes the whole class feel like a game and adds a bit of fun to every assignment, even if the assignment is a heavy dose of treatment.

When can we add competition, real or simulated, into our lessons?

It makes sense to do so any time we can do it with the natural story, like with Racers. A few years ago I created a card game based on activity from iCivics.org to simulate separation of powers in government as outlined in the Constitution. In the original activity students are tasked with building a school lunch menu that satisfies three groups representing the Legislative, Judicial and Executive branches. There is some tension and competition in it, but I wanted more. If we're supposed to have an adversarial system of government, let's make sure the activity is adversarial as well! Though the three groups ultimately had to work together for any of them to be successful, I set specific criteria for each group to "win" the game. I made sure that those criteria overlapped to some degree, but not fully, ensuring they would have to compete to make it work. That made the activity more fun, but it still didn't capture the competitive nature of our government system fully.

I added an additional wrinkle by creating "Political Agenda" cards that each student was trying to accomplish in secret. If they completed their task while the group successfully created a menu they would earn bonus points. For example, I had a Secretary of the Treasury who completed her agenda if the final menu cost less than a certain amount. I had a Junior Senator who had to vote the same way as the Senior Senator did. My personal favorite agenda though was the extreme conservative. His agenda says "You believe the government that governs least, governs best. If no menu is made successfully you win the game." So, unbeknownst to the rest of the players there were two players (the Judicial group had one too) competing to sabotage the whole process. The game gets intense and by the end students can't wait to learn how the government is supposed to work according to the Constitution.

A teacher who found the lesson on my website and used it with their students emailed me to share how it went:

> Good morning! I just wanted to share with you the experience I had with my Juniors and your Lunch Menu activity. Background: I have 3 all-boy-classes of Juniors- they are very hands on, very energetic, and loathe to do book work. When I saw your Lunch Menu activity I was both excited — perhaps this would be a way to channel their energy positively and productively. As soon as I divided them into unequal teams, they were curious as to what was happening. When I gave them the rules, they were quick to figure out what items would best support them getting the most points — their conversations and strategies were great. However, once the menu started getting passed from group to group, the arguments were crazy —, but in that great I'm-learning-but-don't-realize-it way we always strive for. They were yelling back and forth, trying to argue for their individual points as well as for changes to the menu. In one class, the menu went back and forth 4 times! And then, the Cafeteria staff vetoed the final menu, once they saw they weren't getting all the points they wanted, and the young man whose goal was to NOT get the menu approved was laughing and dancing like crazy. I was amazed at the insights they immediately started to get during the debrief. It went so well, I started to record them for my National Boards paper! Thank you for putting that together...it was fantastic.
>
> —Ticey Christenson, Teacher

Plenty of treatment and plenty of treat!

As great as that game is we should remember that games designed specifically for teaching content don't have to be truly competitive. One of my students' favorite games in class is one I created called *Time Warp*. Time Warps are point and click adventure video games like *King's Quest*, *Myst*, or more recently, any of the *TellTale* games like *The Walking Dead* and *Batman*. Students choose a historical character to play and they make decisions for this character as they play out their historical situation. When they choose correctly, the story advances. When they choose incorrectly, they are sent off on a path that requires more reading to ensure they understand the concept. Sometimes though those wrong choices lead to failure (even death!) and they must start the adventure over from the beginning. When that happens, students make a tally mark on their "Adventure Journal" to note the number of times they failed a particular level. This is the illusion of competition. It doesn't actually mean or count for anything if they fail, but the simple act of recording it pushes up the excitement and drama leading to them agonizing over decisions as they click. It's a joy to witness!

I created the first of these games so students could experience the difference in life before and after the Protestant Reformation. They played a series of characters ranging from peasants to monks and played through each scenario twice. In the first they had to try to get through with pre-Reformation norms and rules and the second with post-Reformation changes. The students understood the differences better than they ever had before. At the end of the period many asked when we'd be playing again. I hadn't planned any more, but I knew, based on their reactions, that I had to do more. I ended up making another based on the Age of Exploration and some of the more fantastic journeys undertaken by European explorers. I also made two U.S. history versions for my 8th grade students, one on the Westward movement and another on the lesser known people of the Civil War. Any subject that has multiple stories or perspectives to examine works well. Students absolutely loved them. They were getting plenty of treatment, each had tons of text for students to sift through and analyze, but having a ton of fun.

I made each game using Google Slides. I started by creating a storyboard outlining my overall story and where each branching path might lead. I then turned the story into text slides. Then it was time to add the graphics. Since Slides is fairly limited in how it handles animation, I used animated gifs as much as possible to make the games feel alive. I did use the limited animation tools to time when text boxes and captions would appear, but most of the motion came from the gifs. The final step was to build in the links. Each text box linked to another slide so the story would advance in the proper direction without any interaction on my part. Students could just play and explore at their own pace.

Aside from a little troubleshooting, the students didn't need me at all once the lesson started rolling. With later versions

I created analysis guides for the students to fill out as they played, but I'm not sure they were necessary. Students were intensely engaged as it was, but this helped me focus their attention on the exact content I wanted. One other change I made was to have students start playing in groups. The drama of making a choice was amplified greatly when multiple people had to make it together. Collaboration can be fun too!

Time Warps are big, period long games that require a ton of set up to create, but not all games need to be. Mini-games, small game experiences, can be effective too. In my class we call these Brain Snacks and they are signaled by an animation of a zombie chasing after a brain. I designed them based on research from neuroscientist Judy Willis who, in her book *Research Based Strategies to Ignite Student Learning*, recommends educators switch up brain activity in their students periodically with short, brain-based activities. I drop them in about every 15 minutes during a lecture or just whenever I feel like the room energy is starting to drop. Some of my favorites include "Touch Screen" where students write a word they've learned that day in the air with their finger while a partner tries to guess it, "Switch it Up" where students write three important words from the lesson using both their left and right hands, and "Snowball Fight" where students write a review question on a piece of paper which is then crumpled up and tossed across the room to be answered by someone else. Like some of the other activities above many of them barely qualify as games, but they are definitely fun.

Some are more game-like such as "Mini-game Break!" where students play a shortened version of the trivia review games above that are themed after mini-games from the Super Mario Bros. video game series. They battle ghosts, open random question blocks and try to seek out the proper warp pipes. There are also game-like activities called "Sim It!" where students play a short game to simulate a historical event or concept. One example is a game where students simulate the spread of the Black Death through handshakes (so who knows when this one will ever happen again.) In the first round 3 students are randomly, secretly "infected" while the others mingle. When the "infected" are revealed, without fail, nearly all of the rest of the class is infected as well. In the next round the infected are identified before the handshakes begin. Very quickly they are shunned, even fled from! Their own friends refuse to get anywhere near them. The kids have a great time, but they also quickly, and powerfully, experience the social breakdowns caused by the fear of the Black Death.

It seems, as Mary Poppins famously said, a spoonful of sugar really does help the medicine go down. We can enhance engagement in our classes and programs by adding fun whenever possible. When we do, the treatment doesn't go away or become less important, it just goes down much more easily!

Makin' Memories

Commandment 9: For every ounce of treatment, add a ton of treat
While education is our focus, we should try to make it entertaining by surrounding it with fun.

* * *

Grim Grinning Ghosts
Anything can be made fun! Disney finds fun in topics ranging from dirty pirates to spooky ghosts. Surely we can do the same with assessments, lessons and even worksheets. We don't have to throw out learning to add in fun.

*What is something in your classroom that
you've just accepted won't be fun? How
could you inject some fun into it?*

A Spoonful of Sugar
Sometimes all it takes to make our lessons engaging is a tiny bit of fun. Try adding humor by subverting expectations in absurd ways. One of the best ways is to simply put on a costume.

*What costumes do you have in your closet
already that might work in your classroom?*

The Big Race

Competition is fun! Adding game elements to lessons is an easy way to make them feel like treats and not treatment. Competition can be against other players or against oneself.

What less-than-thrilling lesson can you spice up by adding some competition?

* * *

One Little Spark

"When the subject permits, we let fly with all the satire and gags at our command. Laughter is no enemy to learning."

—Walt Disney

There's a Great Big Beautiful Tomorrow

Build a joke into your lesson. Find something obvious and subvert it with silliness. Put a mustache on Mona Lisa. Have cool modern shades pop up on George Washington's face. Go nuts!

CHAPTER TEN

Keep it Up! (Maintain It)

"In a Disney park or resort, everything must work. Poor maintenance is poor show!"

—Marty Sklar, *Dream It! Do It!*

I've got another confession that some of you really aren't going to like. I know, I know, you almost quit reading after that Indy confession in Chapter 6, but hear me out on this one too!

I really don't like *The Little Mermaid*.

I realize that it almost single-handedly saved the Disney Animation Studios. I know Ariel is one of the most popular Disney princesses. I know the music is incredible. I still don't like it. The core story is one a young girl who disobeys her father, runs away, and gives up her most precious talent all in hopes of meeting a boy she's never spoken to. Yikes. That's not a story I want our kids to emulate! Ursula is the real hero of the story. She's the one who tries to teach Ariel a lesson about foolishly changing yourself for another person!

So, when Ariel's Undersea Adventure opened in Disney California Adventure in 2011, I had no desire to ride it. In fact, I was pretty angry about it. They took out my favorite rest spot to build it! I loved watching the Whoopie Goldberg narrated history of California video that previously played in that spot. The 20-minute video and powerful air-conditioning made for a perfect nap opportunity. No longer.

One very crowded Summer day I found myself on the Boardwalk in the back of the park and desperately in need of a break from the heat. I could walk across the park to the Animation Building, but that would have required expending energy, which I was not in a mood to do. All of the nearby attractions had very long waits (and many of the Boardwalk queue lines are outside!) Ariel's Undersea Adventure did not. Apparently other guests also have good taste. Still, the attraction is indoors, and it had to be better than standing in a crowd in the hot sun. I mean, even my second least-favorite attraction in Disneyland, Snow White's Scary Adventure, now known as Snow White's Enchanted Wish, is worth riding every now and then. (Least favorite? The canoes.) It has short wait lines, is nicely cooled and offers at least some glimpses of entertainment. The Ariel attraction is a similar dark ride so it couldn't be *that* bad, right? Okay, I'll take the plunge.

Almost immediately little extra details began to jump out. The pathway in the queue is speckled with seashells. The picture of Ariel on the wall sparkles with light. The ride vehicle, with the same clam-shell shape of those found in the Haunted Mansion is carved to look like, well, a clam shell. The entrance to the ride tunnel is flanked by the carved wooden planks and detailed hull of a sunken ship. This definitely isn't Snow White's Scary Adventures.

As your clam enters the tunnel an animatronic Scuttle the seagull greets you promising you a great story. Soon, your clam turns around and leans back. This directs your view to the ceiling where a projection of waves of blue light appears. You start to move downhill as you hear the sounds of bubbles. You see the silhouette of Ariel and Flounder swim above you across a projection screen. The effects are simple and subtle, but there's no question what you're experiencing. You're going underwater! This really is an undersea adventure.

The next ride scene shows an animatronic Ariel set in a stunning 3-D recreation of an undersea cave filled with whosits and whatsits galore (and 20 thingamabobs of course.) Just like in the similar scene in the movie, Ariel is singing "Part of Your World." Her lips, eye and body movements are all synced to the music. Unlike the static plywood cutouts of the traditional Fantasyland dark rides, this feels like the film come to life. At this point, I'll admit, I wasn't hating the experience.

Rounding the corner you hear the first few notes of "Under the Sea" just faintly enough to recognize them. The volume grows as you enter a huge scene of sea creatures playing instruments and performing the song. Above you dozens of brightly colored fish swirl and swim. Seahorses dance and play on the tentacles of purple octopus. Audio comes at you from speakers hidden within the figures making it seem like they are truly creating the music. The bass plays the brass, a carp plays a harp, starfish spin, and Ariel dances along joyfully. You are more deeply immersed in color and sound than on any other attraction at the parks. It is overwhelming in all the best ways.

And you're only halfway through the ride! You still get to see the massive, fully animated recreation of Ursula, simulated dancing waterspouts and brilliant LED fireworks before your adventure ends. It's impressive.

The effort the Imagineers put into making Ariel's Undersea Adventure the very best dark ride it could be has made it one of my favorite attractions despite my dislike for the source material. It is a true testament to the value of putting one's all into a project.

* * *

The Courageous Creativity Conference I've mentioned previously is an annual conference at Disneyland for arts educators, originally inspired by Marty Sklar. It is organized by a partnership between Disney Imagineering and the California Arts Project. It promises teachers the opportunity to hear from Disney Imagineers both active and retired. I'm not an art teacher, but this was an opportunity I was not going to miss! For three days not only was I given access to great ideas from some of the world's most creative minds, but I was treated like a king. I have never felt more appreciated as an educator than at these conferences. The food was stellar, each event started on time and every single Disney cast member was gracious and professional. The conference is a perfect example of Disney's focus on ensuring everything works for their guests.

At the 2019 conference I asked the panel of Imagineers if they had advice on how we teachers could bring Imagineering magic into our classrooms. Imagineer Dex Tanksley said, "Treat every day like it was your first day." His point was that all the passion, energy, excitement and planning we put into our first day of any task is what we should be trying to match every day. This should make perfect sense for teachers. We get

a new "first day" every year! I put more into making that first
day magical than any other. I've long said I want my first day
to be my best day. If I followed his advice and made each day
like my first day, then every day would be my best day!

As much as I love his answer, it was not what I was expecting. I was expecting some practical tips I could implement.
Dex, for example, was trained as an architect. Aren't they
known for being practical? I should have known better. Dex
isn't just an architect. He's an Imagineer! Plus, Marty Sklar
gave very similar advice in his book when he said, "Even the
most mundane job must be done with skill and enthusiasm
to maintain those Disney standards. You do it the best way
you know how — with panache and gusto! You must keep
it up — every day — because that day may be the only day
a family visits." That is a perfect summation of the ideas in
Commandment 10: Keep it up! (Maintain it!) If we're going
to put in the work to make a magical experience one day, we
should also work to keep that level of magic up daily.

That's obviously quite a challenge. I find it far too easy to
fall into a routine in the classroom and let the little things
slide by. My desk starts the year clean and by the end of week
one I've got piles of papers, notes to myself, staplers, pens and
goodness knows what else strewn about. By the end of week
two those piles have spread all over the room! I'd like to say
I don't know how it happens, but I do. I make little compro-
mises or say to myself "I'll get to that later." and when I don't, I
leave it for the next day. I don't do the daily maintenance that
I ought to do. I'm getting better at it, but I've got a long way to
go to match Disneyland!

Their daily maintenance routine is astounding and everyone plays a part, not just the custodial staff. The park is always
clean and orderly. Horses walk up and down Main Street,
U.S.A. all day doing things that horses must do, but you'd never
know it. Guests drop popcorn, spill ice cream and spit gum
out on the ground, but again, you'd never know it. Messes are
cleaned up immediately by custodians, random cast members
or even the sharply dressed managers roaming the park with
their ubiquitous garbage-grabbing arm extenders. This emphasis on cleanliness subconsciously encourages guests to do the

same. Disney guests certainly aren't perfect, but they regularly pick up trash and clean up their own messes because it just feels natural in a place like Disneyland. I probably shouldn't get so upset at the misplaced rulers, torn paper edges and left behind pencils that pepper my room at the end of each day. I'm the one who failed to set the right tone by keeping up! Schools and classrooms that ignore this maintenance encourage their students to care little about their environment.

There's another aspect of maintenance that I've found is ignored regularly in classrooms — technology maintenance. For Disney this is a problem that can't be ignored. As noted previously, their primary company value is safety. Everything they design or do must first and foremost be safe. I remember Disney Vice President of Live Entertainment Matt Conover saying that the phrase "one in a million" means nothing to Disney. If something can go wrong one in a million times that means it would go wrong dozens or hundreds of times in a typical year at Disneyland and that is simply unacceptable. If a ride mechanism fails even once it could be catastrophic and lead to serious injuries or worse. It puts that core value of safety at great risk. As a result, Disney projects are designed to much higher specifications than one in a million! Keeping those projects running smoothly and safely through mainte-nance then is of the utmost importance. Safety checks on their technology are constant, just like the cleanliness ones.

Technology maintenance is also important to the show itself. A motionless animatronic may not be a safety hazard, but it certainly stands out. A light flickering or completely out will draw attention away from a dozen things that are working properly. Anything like this distracts from the guest experience.

While failing technology may not be a safety issue for us it can completely ruin our classroom show and is something we must keep up. You've surely experienced a show ruined by failed technology yourself. I know I've attended far too many professional development workshops and education conferences where the speaker can't get his slideshow up on the screen or a planned YouTube video to play. In these situa-tions, it's easy to blame the technology of the venue (it's always the wi-fi!), but still you hear the giggles and sighs around the room whenever this happens. It causes me to immediately lose some faith in the presenter and I know I'm not alone. If the presenter didn't value my time enough to prepare their show why should I value what they have to say? It is cynical I know, but it is human.

Technology should be tested before show time! In our classrooms we really can't (or shouldn't) make the same excuses blaming the venue. We have home court advantage! Of course, things go wrong with technology in our schools, but we should at least be aware of it even if we can't fix it. I test every tech tool I plan to use the morning before I use it with my students, even things I've done for years and years. You simply never know if your network will go down or if the night custodian bumped a cord and loosened a connection. It's up to us to test, test, and re-test our technology to make sure our classroom show is good. Marty put it this way, "Poor maintenance is poor show and poor show is unacceptable in the Disney experience." As much as it is in our power, we need to make sure our technology is functioning properly. We'll still have hiccups, but it shouldn't be because we were unprepared!

We should not, however, let the risk of failure stop us from learning and trying new things, including technology. Lee Cockerell, said, "As we say at Disney, 'In times of drastic change it is the learners who inherit the future.'" Unfortunately, as noted above, sometimes professional development for teachers is not particularly effective. Far too often it is the next-big-thing presented in the same way as the last five next-big-things that were really just repackaging of a next-big-thing from ten years ago. The presenters sometimes haven't been in a classroom for years, if at all. It is sadly common that in a two day training I walk away with only one or two ideas even worth pursuing and when I do buy in and try the ideas they frequently fall way short of the rosy picture painted by the trainer.

So, where do we go to be learners? Each other! We live in a time when connecting with other teachers is easier than ever before. Today, nearly all of my great new ideas come from fellow teachers on Twitter. For example, I recently tired of once again trying to find a way to make the myriad causes of the Fall of the Roman Empire make sense to my 7th graders. I have approximately two days to teach the topic and I've never quite been happy with it. I designed a decision-making game (thanks chapter 9!) which helped, but it was still quite conceptually advanced. I wanted something simple. I asked my followers on Twitter and added the Social Studies Chat hashtag (#sschat) and within a couple hours (on the Sunday of Labor Day weekend no less) I had more than half a dozen ideas ranging from DBQs, to a Cause and Effect poster activity, to my favorite, a game of Jenga where the pieces represent the things missing as Rome weakened and paper balls become the outside forces threatening to topple the tower.

Nearly all of the ideas were shared freely by other teachers. They didn't come from corporate representatives with an agenda. Admittedly, sometimes teachers are looking to sell things to you too, but there are plenty more out there who realize we are in this together for all of our kids and are more than happy to share. If you're new to Twitter, I suggest just jumping into a chat. There are plenty out there for teachers ranging from general ones like #edchat (one of the busiest and therefore most commercial tags unfortunately) and #tlap (Teach Like a Pirate) to subject specific ones like #sschat and even those dedicated to more focused topics like using games in education like #games4ed. Join in and add your voice!

Constant learning and growth leads to the true focus of this commandment. Maintaining the high standards we set at the start of a year is important, but it is even more important to always look to improve the experience in our classrooms. At 2018's Courageous Creativity Conference the opening keynote speech, which was given by Marty Sklar until his passing in 2017, was delivered by Matt Conover. His one-hour speech was filled with Imagineering wisdom and Disney magic, but one line in particular stood out to me more than any other. Matt said that the chief design philosophy at Disney Live Entertainment was pretty simple, "No experience is too small to be excellent." He talked about some of the little things Disney Entertainment did such as putting video screens in the inside facing rooms on the Disney Cruise Ships that had a live feed of the ocean outside so even those without a balcony room could experience the beauty of the voyage. Disney is always looking to improve their guests' experiences even when they are already rated as providing the best in class.

I mentioned how the Imagineers ensure even the most basic of objects like walkways are designed to enhance the story of various lands. We also looked at how even the visual designs of the queue lines at Disneyland are carefully and thoughtfully planned. The final section of the line to Space Mountain, which I mentioned back in chapter 3, for example, winds through futuristic looking tunnels before opening up to show a massive spaceship. The queue for Disneyland's newest attraction, Rise of the Resistance, is so well designed that it literally is part of the attraction. It is definitely excellent!

Matt's comment hit me hard. I immediately thought over all the things I do with students on a given day and how many of them fall short of excellence. For example, I start each day with a bellwork activity. It is important to get students into an academic mindset immediately. The activities are simple and largely uninteresting. It might be a simple thought question or adding summaries to the previous day's notes. Honestly, in most cases, it is something I come up with at the last minute. Almost certainly as a result, it is rarely excellent. Matt's comment caused me to reevaluate this basic process and ask myself how I could improve it.

For the last year I've refocused on ensuring my bellwork is a time for previewing the lesson and building excitement, not just to set an academic mood. That's still important, but I look at it now as the queue time for the attraction — an opportunity to build up the experience before it truly begins. In the past, my bellwork has connected to the story to some degree, but never in any deep (or excellent) capacity. Further, it never looked excellent. It was always just a whole bunch of words on the screen with no visual connection to the story of the day. Fixing 175 different activities and slides has been a daunting task. In fact, it has been an impossible one. I've so far only managed to improve about one a week, but it's a start.

No experience is too small to be excellent!

Plussing

In Disney speak the regular improvement of the parks and attractions is known as plussing. It is the idea that we should always be improving. This means accepting the idea that our design work is never done. The good news is that plussing does not mean you have to start from scratch! Plussing can happen by simply adding to whatever you already have. Some of our lessons are great already and need just a little bit of a push to be excellent (or more excellent!) In 2014 the Disney Imagineers set to work updating one of the park's most consistently popular attractions, Alice in Wonderland. The attraction is constantly busy, often running second in Fantasyland wait times only behind the always lengthy wait for Peter Pan's Flight. It certainly didn't need to be updated. Other attractions went far longer without any updates, yet the Disney Imagineers updated it anyway giving us a perfect example of why we should improve even those lessons we feel are great — they can always be better!

The changes made were relatively small. The Imagineers replaced some lightly animated sculpted characters with projected animations. This is similar to the technology used on a smaller scale in a similar attraction, The Many Adventures of Winnie the Pooh, which opened in 2003. These updated ride scenes, which blend perfectly with the rest of the attraction, make it feel even more like you are riding through the scenes of the movie rather than simply seeing them recreated in sculpture. Other small technological enhancements were made to make the attraction feel modern and not like one built in 1983.

I would call this incremental plussing, small enhancements to improve an existing project bit by bit. Similar changes using projection technology were made to Big Thunder Mountain Railroad, Pirates of the Caribbean and even Space Mountain as it became Hyperspace Mountain. All were clearly popular attractions already, but now the attractions are better and more alive than they have ever been.

Over the course of my 15 plus years of teaching I've been able to make many small enhancements using technology. I started with PowerPoint displayed on a CRT television through the old red, yellow and white composite cables. It was so blurry that any font size below 40 was unreadable. (It didn't help that I hadn't yet learned the importance of Commandment 5 and my presentations were heavy on textual literacy, not visual.) The sound was equally awful coming through a TV speaker at the front of the room. Sorry if you're sitting in the back! It seemed to work well at the time, in fact, it was cutting edge! The simple fact that I wasn't showing a hand-written transparency on an overhead projector was enough to amaze my students. If I did the same today I wouldn't hold their attention for more than a couple minutes.

Within a few years I'd purchased an LCD projector. It was bulky and the resolution was far from great (though much better than a 36-inch CRT television!) It sat on top of a cart previously used for an overhead projector. I hooked up a set of very basic, very underpowered computer speakers to it and placed those on the cart as well. They didn't sound great but, again, they were better than the speakers on the old television (still sorry to those who sat in the back!) This new set up not only improved the general show, but it opened up new avenues for me to explore in design. Not having to use 40-point fonts gave me screen space to use many more visuals than I had before, which made the shows much more engaging.

In the years since, I've continued to keep up with technology in my classroom. The projector is now mounted with an even larger screen. The sound comes out of speakers in the ceiling, so it is evenly distributed throughout the space. I've added small touches like custom lighting and Bluetooth speakers to add flair and uniqueness to certain labs. The lights can look like waves on the ceiling when we do our Sunken Ship investigation. Black lights can make the glow-in-the-dark stars on the ceiling light up leading to clues in Breakout activities. The Bluetooth speakers can add directional audio like in my Vicksburg Siege activity where cannons seemingly fire from many directions and a dog walks through the cave where we are hiding. I'm still in a space that was built in 1951, but keeping up with technology allows me to put on a show that helps it feel much more modern and to keep my activities feeling fresh even after many years.

Sometimes we don't have the opportunity (or funding) to "plus" using technology the way I've been able to. Thankfully, there are plenty of other ways we can do so, and it doesn't have to be very drastic. We can change fonts on worksheets or better separate out sections with boxes to make them easier to read. We can use any of the techniques we've discussed in previous chapters to update existing lessons, not just to create brand new ones. Whenever we add more treat or more story to a lesson we are plussing it. If we consistently make those incremental plusses eventually everything is going to be excellent.

Plussing can also take larger steps forward. Even when we want something to feel completely new we can build on those things we've already designed to make the creation process easier. I would call this transitional plussing. One great example is the Inside Out: Emotional Whirlwind attraction that opened in Disney California Adventure in 2019. The attraction was placed into the Pixar Pier area in the back of the park. It took the place of Maliboomer which was removed in 2010. That spot sat empty for the next nine years — an area ripe for plussing! When the entire Boardwalk area was plussed to become Pixar Pier it made sense to include an attraction based on *Inside Out* (since it is the greatest movie ever made.) A Bug's Land, based on the Pixar film *A Bug's Life,* had recently closed. Disney could have transplanted one of the attractions from that land to Pixar Pier and it would have fit the general theme. However, *A Bug's Life* came out in 1998. It has lost some of its relevance and popularity. Just moving an old attraction from an aging movie would fulfill the need, but it might not be excellent.

The Disney Imagineers made a brilliant decision. They took one of the attractions from A Bug's Land, Flik's Flyers, and plussed it. It was rethemed around the characters and themes of *Inside Out*. What were once hot air balloons made of bug-friendly materials are now balloons held aloft by the stored memory orbs from the movie. They built a backdrop showing the memory bank scene from the film and included detailed sculptures of each of the characters from the movie as well. They also wrote new music for the attraction based on the different emotions in the film. Each run of the attraction plays a different song showing how different emotions can be in control at different times — a key theme of the movie. Observant guests may well recognize it is just a re-themed version of Flik's Flyers, but it is clearly an upgrade and is now definitely excellent!

My History Mystery activities which I introduced in chapter 4 take significantly more time to design and build than any other lesson I do. The first one that I made along with colleagues was the investigation into the Medici assassination in the late 1400s. It began as a text-based activity. Students read a series of short passages at 8 different stations that represented different points of view on the investigation. Making sure the stations were balanced in length and played off of one another proved challenging, but we got there. Then we plussed each station to make them appear more real. For example, we took one that included information about possible involvement by the Duke of Urbino and, using the *CrazyTalk* program I mentioned, turned it into a talking portrait of the Duke proclaiming his innocence. We took some information about the Pazzi family and made it look like an official court deposition. A discussion of Medici influence in Florence became a fake newspaper article. We did all we could to turn those boring reading stations into real looking artifacts. It was a ton of work, but made the lab incredible. Students are highly engaged during the investigation process and can't wait to write their evidence-based arguments as a conclusion.

Yet, the thought of doing another lab like this from scratch was daunting. As good as it was, was it really worth all the work? Was it really *that* much better than the text version? Yes, it was, but thankfully, creating the next one would take far less work. When I started building another investigation, this time on the causes of the collapse of the Mayan Empire, I already had a base to work from. I used the exact same analysis guide and presentation format that I did for the Medici version and just changed the questions. I was also able to use the "real" evidence from the Medici lab as templates for the Mayan one. The autopsy report, for example, was just a matter of changing a few details like cause and time of death. It was still a lot of work to build, but far easier than the first time. Using the same general set up and adaptation of existing evidence has allowed me to create more History Mystery labs including some for U.S. history as well. It gets easier and faster each time. Making the transition from that original lab to many other topics has allowed me to bring this powerful experience to my students multiple times throughout the year without too much work on my part.

Sometimes though you need an entirely new attraction. Early on in my career I worked closely with a few colleagues to create a set of lesson types for social studies. We wanted to create more lessons like History Mysteries that we could use as templates for multiple units throughout the year. We found it rather stunning that nothing like this was available at the time. With a Google search one could find a handful of pretty boring PowerPoint presentations, plenty of worksheets and, with luck, a one-off project or inquiry activity. The latter is what we wanted in our classrooms, but the thought of having to design from scratch each time was not something any of us were eager to pursue. If we could create 5-10 lesson types we could then just reuse those with new topics in each unit. That sounds much more doable. It took years, but we did it.

When we started building these new lesson types we didn't want to start from scratch, but we also didn't want to just make more History Mysteries. We took that concept and transformed it into something that felt new using similar setup and strategies. I'll call this transformational plussing. Ariel's Undersea Adventure is the perfect example. This attraction is similar in style and design to the Fantasyland dark rides like Peter Pan's Flight that have been around for decades, but it has modern features that make the attraction far more immersive. In these dark rides you sit in a ride vehicle and are carried through "scenes" from the movie which are recreated using, primarily, animatronic figures. Unlike many of the older dark rides that miss large swaths of the story or just end out of nowhere (Snow White's Scary Adventures I'm looking at you), this attraction truly captures the whole of the Little Mermaid story. The animatronic characters are more expressive with seemingly dozens of more points of articulation. The setting is better represented as you dive under the water thanks to some impressive projection technology. As Imagineer Joe Harrington said, "With each new attraction we add new tools to our storytelling toolbox, but our guests don't notice those cool tech tools. Instead, they are living our stories and loving it." It's a dark ride, but feels entirely new.

The inspiration I needed to create a new type of mystery came when I stumbled upon an idea at Docsteach.org from the National Archives that visually represented argumentative evidence on a balance. I now had my "technology" to make it feel different. I created a similar mystery, this time built around the question of whether Robin Hood was a real person or completely made up. It still had exhibits for students to analyze and still had an argumentative paragraph at the end. I changed the way that students were to analyze the evidence. In the newly named Weigh the Evidence students would assign a numerical value ranging from -2 to +2 simulating the balance idea, to measure the value of each exhibit in terms of answering an essential question. Students are asked to consider the source, relevance and accuracy of the information. That happens with History Mystery as well, but not in an explicit manner.

In some ways the lab just felt like a History Mystery with more work and less role play. In the eyes of my students I had "minussed" the activity, not plussed it! I was very happy with the improved, or at least different, learning focus driven by this new "technology", but it needed something just a little more to make it feel unique. If it didn't feel as much like a History Mystery, but instead like something entirely new, then it wouldn't be subject to quite the same level of comparison. So, I changed the track layout... in a sense. Instead of placing the exhibits around the room I put them all on the screen. We'd go through them together with lots of discussion and pair-sharing throughout. This would be a linear experience whereas History Mysteries are much more open and free flowing. The tweak worked. All of a sudden Weigh the Evidence felt like a completely different activity. I made just two structural changes, but it bought me six more lessons over the course of the year. If I had made 6 more History Mysteries, then burnout due to oversaturation was a very likely result, but not when I plussed it to make something new.

To create a Weigh the Evidence you start with a two-sided question. I have questions like "Did Rome leave a positive legacy?" "Does George Washington deserve to be honored on the one-dollar bill?" and "Were Ninjas real?" It works for any subject or topic requiring evidence-based writing. You then gather 5-6 evidence sources with varying reliability and conclusions. I've found for my 7th graders 5 is pretty much the magic number we can reasonably finish in a class period. For evidence I've used excerpts from primary sources, quotes from modern secondary sources, photographs, maps, clips from YouTube videos and even clips from fictional Hollywood movies (my favorite is a ridiculous clip from Mel Brooks' *Robin Hood: Men in Tights*.) Since part of the purpose of the activity is to evaluate source validity it makes sense to use an invalid source here and there. When students rate the exhibits these invalid sources receive a score of zero. They do not contribute to either side of the argument. Next, I arrange the sources into a slideshow presentation which includes sentence frames for their final argumentative paragraph. When possible I make a video intro to build hype and excitement. Aside from the video, the setup is remarkably easy.

Running the activity, especially the first couple times with 7th graders is a bit more challenging. The first problem I ran into, quite unexpectedly, is that many of my students at that point don't understand how to work with integers. When they reached the "add up your points step" they honestly couldn't do it. I learned to avoid this problem by having them record their answers on a Google Sheet which does the math for them. After the intro video I show the first exhibit and give them a couple minutes to record their number value and explanation of why. A negative score indicates support for the "no" side of the argument while a positive means it supports "yes." As I said, a zero means it isn't useful in supporting either side. It is very important to have students share with a partner after writing. Rating evidence in this way is very unfamiliar to students and hearing other opinions is important in helping them improve their evaluations.

I now had two different lesson types I could use for each unit. That's 12 teaching days, nearly 10% of the year! I loved how these worked, but I was a bit leery of dipping into the well again. I now had two labs with very similar opening, middle and concluding segments. Each had aspects that made them unique enough to slide by 12 times, but could I make another and try for 18?

I mentioned back in Chapter 2 how a colleague kept telling me about an introductory investigation he had made for our Mayan unit called Digging for the Truth. It sounded very similar to Weigh the Evidence. It used a series of images of artifacts to lead students to forming some initial hypotheses about a civilization. It didn't have the number rating mechanic, but it still seemed so similar that I hesitated to try it. Thankfully, I finally gave in and did. Though it looked very similar in presentation, the simple act of changing the focus for students from answering a question to exploring an unknown world made it feel entirely different. I made a few small tweaks like adding a scripted narrative to help feed the exploration feel and I had a model for lessons 13 to 18, but it was time for something new.

Sometimes creating something new and better is a matter of just combining the best parts of things you've done before. One of Imagineering's crowning achievements is the Radiator Springs Racers attraction which opened in 2012 at Disney California Adventure. The attraction is a combination of all the best things Disney has created before. It is heavily themed and story driven like the dark rides and offers intense excitement like the thrill rides. It really feels like two different attractions in one. The first half is a peaceful drive through Ornament Valley while the second is a breakneck race simulating the old slot car toys. It's like you get to ride Peter Pan's Flight and Big Thunder Mountain all in one attraction!

Throughout the attraction there are incredible details that put it above just about any other. One simply cannot miss the stunning scenery the Imagineers built around the attraction. The mountainous rock formations tower over the park from the second you walk in the entrance gate. Getting a close-up tour of them while riding the attraction is awe inspiring. The sound, which is blasted directly into your ears like on Space Mountain, is a constant companion on the journey setting the mood better than any other attraction at the California parks (sorry Haunted Mansion.) Riding at night you are treated to stunning lighting effects that illuminate the entire mountain range and masterful visual communication through the various road signs throughout the attraction. It really is a perfect example of taking every tool you've built or used and putting them together to make something amazing.

In early 2019 I decided it was time to make my own Radiator Springs Racers for my students. I wanted to do something big with all the new skills, tricks and great Imagineering advice I'd learned over the years. I just couldn't find the right topic. Then, someone on Twitter asked for a Breakout activity based on the Underground Railroad. When nobody could find one, I realized I had my topic. I put myself to work immediately. I'd made a few Breakouts before and they were good, but I mostly just stuck to the Breakout EDU model and formula — a series of fairly basic, often digital, puzzles that lead to a locked box. I plussed my Washington's Spy Ring version by using some of the same codes and cyphers that the spy ring really used. I plussed my Constitution one by adding a larger wrapping narrative and having the final reward be a copy of the "ultimate weapon against tyranny!" — the Constitution. For this one I wanted to really push the limits of what a Breakout could look like.

My first thought was to take the "real artifacts" aspect of the History Mystery labs. One of the coolest things about them is when kids ask me "Is this real?" in reference to our recreated fakes. I wanted that element. I began by purchasing an old-fashioned camping lantern. That would be turned on and hang outside above my door as one of the clues. One of the most legendary signs of the Underground Railroad was a house across the Ohio River which had a lantern hanging out front. Supposedly if the light was on it was safe for escapees to cross the river. If it was off it meant to wait. I put the lantern outside the day before the activity with the light off and didn't say anything about it. The next day, the light was on. As students read through the background information for the activity I heard many throughout the day say "oooh, that's why there was a lantern outside!"

Next, a colleague of mine mentioned that he had a bunch of "slave bags" from Colonial Williamsburg that had been in a closet for years. Each bag was filled with real objects a slave might be able to obtain like a shell and a cloth sock. Perfect! I created two puzzles built around the objects in the bag. Students would have to deeply analyze each item to figure them out. When they received their clue packs they all immediately went to the bag. This was a definite plus over many of the other activities in class which just have reading and maybe a printed graphic or two. "Forget reading, there's real stuff here!"

The next step was to create a narrative hook and a video to introduce it. I did not want the students to be playing as members of the railroad. Some topics just shouldn't be role-played and slavery, even resistance to it, is right at the top of the list. So, I instead used our already existing Fracture Crisis story and made them agents in a fictional future world serving as resistance fighters in a recently conquered United States. They would learn about the routes and codes used by the Underground Railroad in order to help fellow trapped agents escape. I then made an introduction video to help build interest and set the proper tone. I learned that a television show about the Underground Railroad had come out recently called *Underground*. I started watching it and the opening scene provided the perfect visuals for the activity. The audio, however, was not what I wanted. I was stuck on finding the right tone until I took a break to play video games. I turned on my Xbox to play some *Warframe* and the opening song, *We All Lift Together*, hit me. It is a modern take on an old railway worker song. It was perfect.

I reorganized the opening scene and credits from the television show and arranged it all in time with the music. I finished the narrative angle with a new title, *Resistance: Underground* (which led to me plussing all of my Breakouts by making them into Resistance stories.)

I was fairly happy with everything, but it was still missing that final piece. It was missing those incredible mountains that surround Radiator Springs. It was then that I took advantage of the best plussing tool available to any of us — collaboration. Another colleague of mine came up with the brilliant idea of using the aforementioned glowing star stickers on the ceiling to form the Big Dipper which the Underground Railroad is alleged to have used as a guide for escaping slaves. Now that is plussing! I put the stickers up and made a clue about how "night would reveal the path to freedom." I shut the lights off and... well, nothing really. They barely glowed. I remembered other teachers mentioning how they had used black light flashlights with invisible ink in their Breakouts and I figured I'd try that. I bought one to test on the stickers. It worked perfectly. They lit up just as I'd hoped. I immediately ordered one for each group. I now had my final puzzle and it would be unlike anything they'd done before. That's what it means to keep it up!

The students loved the lab. They were engaged throughout. I had students who don't typically put their all into their work leading their teams in ways I never thought possible. Seeing the reaction of the winning group when they first lit up the stars on the ceiling is something I'll never forget. At the end students couldn't wait to dig deeper and learn about this important part of our history.

So, where can we go for inspiration to make those constant changes? Thankfully, we live in a time when inspiration, ideas and collaboration are only a few clicks away. A couple times this chapter I've mentioned how I've found ideas and support from other educators on Twitter. In many ways Twitter has become the primary source of professional development for many educators. Whether it's through scheduled chats or just building up a "Personal Learning Network" of other educators to follow, there is plenty of opportunity for inspiration.

Despite all the focus on technology books are still great for inspiration too. I mentioned *Teach Like a Pirate* by Dave Burgess in an earlier chapter and I can't recommend it enough. It is the book I wish I'd been given as a new teacher alongside *The First Days of School*. The focus of the book is on providing ideas to "hook" students in learning activities. The first half outlines many ways Dave did it in his class and the second features a series of questions you can ask yourself to create hooks for your own lessons. Just seeing what is possible can be a huge inspiration. Some other great books to check out with this in mind are Jane McGonigal's *Reality is Broken* and of course, my inspiration for this book, Marty Sklar's *One Little Spark: Mickey's Ten Commandments and the Road to Imagineering.* All three have inspired me greatly as a teacher and creator and I think they will inspire you too.

Or, of course, you could always spend a day at Disneyland! There's never a day I leave the park without thinking about something from my day that I want to bring into my classroom!

Maintaining high levels of polish, creativity and fun in your classroom isn't easy, but it is worth it. Our lessons and students are not finished products. As our students grow and change so should our lessons. Walt Disney took great joy in the fact that Disneyland was different from his films. Those films, once finished, could not be changed. They were done. Disneyland though was much different. Walt put it this way, "Disneyland is something that will never be finished. It's alive. It will be a living, breathing thing that will need change. A picture is a thing, once you wrap it up and turn it over to Technicolor, you're through. I wanted something alive, something that could grow. Not only can I add things, but even the trees will grow and become more beautiful each year."

We, on the other hand, have the opportunity to start fresh every single year. Our classrooms too can grow and become more beautiful each year. Keep it up!

Makin' Memories

Commandment 10: Keep it up (Maintain it!)
Aim to keep high standards every day and keep pushing to do even better.

Be Prepared

Think about how much preparation we put into our first day. We arrange, decorate and clean our classrooms. We wear our nicest clothes. If we want to keep it up, we have to prepare like this as often as possible. Test your technology, organize your classroom and set the tone daily.

*How can you build technology test-
runs into your daily routine?*

Try Everything

"Keep it up!" is a call to keep growing as a teacher. Keep trying new things! Add new bells and whistles to an old lesson, use an old lesson as a model for something new or build something entirely from the ground up using the best parts of your other lessons.

What is something new you've seen in entertainment media that you could bring into your classroom?

Almost There

The idea that perfection is always just out of reach can be overwhelming. Just remember, you know where you're going, and gettin' closer every day! Keep moving forward!

*What is a goal you've let slip away
because it seemed too far away?*

* * *

One Little Spark

"Disneyland will never be completed, as long
as there is imagination left in the world."

—Walt Disney

There's a Great Big Beautiful Tomorrow

Treat tomorrow like your first day of the year. Dress in your
first day clothes and put on your best welcome smile!

Conclusion

When I began writing this book I did so with the intent to focus solely on improving lesson design and visual presentation using Imagineering techniques. I came in with the idea that a perfectly designed experience would be all it took to turn a classroom into Disneyland. I was wrong. The more I researched, particularly Marty Sklar himself, the more I realized that personal authenticity, spending time with your audience and being a mentor are all huge parts of making your classroom magical. Only when our students know we care and that we truly value their opinions, beliefs and goals will they buy into the experiences we design for them. That became the true story of this book. (At least that means there is room for a sequel!)

Now it's time to say goodbye...

As I said, whenever I leave Disneyland, I go away inspired. I notice so many things that I rushed past on the way in (got to get to Space Mountain before the line gets too long!) I see the windows on Main Street, U.S.A. painted with the names of Imagineering legends like Bob Gurr and Marc Davis — almost like the credits at the end of a movie. I marvel at the living-window displays in the Emporium before catching a last glimpse of Walt's lantern in the window above the fire station. I get another look at the attraction posters as I walk through the tunnel transition and back out into the entrance lobby. I pass through the exit turnstiles and take one last glance at my name etched into my brick and head out toward the tram that takes me to my car as the joyful, Disney-themed music slowly fades out.

To all our company...

Admittedly, I also walk away tired. That final trek to the tram is a slog as shoulders slump and aching feet drag. That tram ride back to the parking area is often deathly silent. The sound of pure exhaustion. What I've presented in this book is a great challenge and potentially an exhausting one. It is the challenge faced by many creators. Even the incredibly accomplished artist Leonardo Da Vinci was never satisfied with his own work and thus rarely finished anything. When I started teaching, I planned to have all of my lessons created, tested and perfected by the end of year three. As I found myself changing my lessons every year that plan quickly became year 5. Then, thankfully, I realized I'd never be done. New students, new ideas and new technology would, and should, always be coming into my classroom — just like Disneyland.

M — I — C...

However, it's easy to feel "done" as a teacher. It's easy to hesitate to add to our program when we are constantly introduced to the latest "next big thing" every couple of years. It's easy to give up when policy decisions are made above our heads that we know are not good for kids. We see, and feel, the negative effects of those policies on a daily basis. In light of all that it's easy to say what we're doing is good enough. Good enough isn't Disney and it certainly isn't Imagineering. Being excellent is hard. If it was easy everyone would do it.

See you real soon...

We're professionals. Our profession matters. We got into this career to change lives, to share our passions and to build the future. Those aspirations cannot be met without thoughtful planning, deep preparation, and dynamic presentation. Mickey's Ten Commandments, though written for theme park design, give us the tools to meet those targets. We must know our audience, design with their needs in mind and push to exceed their expectations daily — just like the Imagineers do.

K — E — Y...

We can do this if we work together. I share all the lessons I create for free online. Even if none of them directly apply to your content area, I hope you can take ideas from them or at least use them as a template for your own. Don't reinvent the wheel! So many of my ideas have come through inspiration from others. I wouldn't be the teacher I am today, and my students certainly wouldn't have the experiences they have today if I had to do this all alone. Education shouldn't be about one-upping one another. It should be about one-upping *ourselves*! If one of us designs a lesson that motivates and engages our 30 to 200 students, shouldn't we want *every* student to have access to that same experience? Of course. So, get out there and share!

Why? Because we like you!

Thank you for taking this journey with me. This all started with one little spark five years ago when I read... well... *One Little Spark*. It helped put into words and sequence so many of the ideas I've juggled around in my head throughout my career. It drove me to dive into historical research unlike any I've done before. Thank you to my family, especially my mom, who has had to endure countless "fun facts" from me that I picked up during that research on our regular trips to Disneyland. Thank you to Marty Sklar for being the heart and soul of such an incredible group of people. Thank you to my colleagues who have helped me create all these activities. Thank you to my supporters who showed so much interest in this book idea every time I mentioned it. Lastly, thank you to you. If you've read this far you are surely willing to push yourself to provide your students with the most magical experiences you can. That deserves to be recognized and thanked.

M-O-U-S-E.

Let's teach with magic!

Bibliography

Cockerell, Lee. *Creating Magic: 10 Common Sense Leadership Strategies from a Life at Disney.* Currency, 2008.

Dening, Lizzy. "What Lies beneath: Going Underground to Uncover Disney World's Deepest Secrets." *Daily Mail*, 7 Jan. 2014, www.dailymail.co.uk/travel/article-2533335/The-secrets-Disney-World-Florida-Going-underground-Orlando.html

France, Van Arsdale. *Window on Main Street: 35 Years of Creating Happiness at Disneyland Park.* Theme Park Press, 2013.

Gennawey, Sam. *The Disneyland Story: The Unofficial Guide to the Evolution of Walt Disney's Dream.* Keen Communications, 2014.

Grant, S.G. "From Inquiry Arc to Instructional Practice: The Potential of the C3 Framework." *Social Education* 77(6). 2013.

Hench, John. *Designing Disney: Imagineering and the Art of the Show. Disney Editions,* 2003.

Lipp, Doug. *Disney U: How Disney University Develops the World's Most Engaged, Loyal, and Customer-Centric Employees.* McGraw Hill Education, 2013.

Martin, Hugo. "They're Disneyland Superfans: Why a Lawsuit is Alleging Gangster-like Tactics Against One Social Club." *Los Angeles Times*, 9 Feb. 2018. https://www.latimes.com/business/la-fi-disneyland-social-clubs-20180209-story.html.

Mumpower, David. "The Murky History of Disney's Jungle Cruise." *Themeparktourist.com.* 31 Aug. 2015. https://www.themeparktourist.com/features/20150821/30496/jungle-cruise-amazon-adventure-orange-grove?page=3

Rafferty, Kevin. *Magic Journey: My Fantastical Walt Disney Imagineering Career.* Disney Editions, 2019.

Reisman, Avishag, Ph.D. & Sam Wineburg, Ph.D. "Text Complexity" in the History Classroom: Teaching to and Beyond the Common Core." *Social Studies Review* 2012.

Sklar, Marty. *Dream It! Do It!: My Half-Century Creating Disney's Magic Kingdoms; the People, the Places, the Projects.* Disney Editions, 2013.

Sklar, Marty. *Travels with Figment: On the Road in Search of Disney Dreams.* Disney Editions, 2019.

Sklar, Marty, and Leslie Sklar. *One Little Spark!: Mickey's Ten Commandments and the Road to Imagineering.* Disney Editions, 2015.

The Disney Institute. *Be Our Guest: Perfecting the Art of Customer Service.* Disney Editions, 2011.

The Imagineering Way: Ideas to Ignite Your Creativity. Disney Editions, 2003.

Testimonials

There are three things you need to be the most creative and successful person you can be, they are, Education, Experience and Exposure. *Teach with Magic* will show you how to teach and learn with magic day in and day out. The more you know, the more creative and successful you will become.

—Lee Cockerell, Executive Vice President (Retired and Inspired) Walt Disney World Resort and author of *Creating Magic...Ten Common Sense Leadership Strategies from a Life at Disney.*

A delightful read that will not only conjure up memories, but will spark ideas, create change, and produce joy in students and teachers alike in classrooms around the world. This book is laid out to help make your class a walk in the park. Theme park, that is! Prepare to step into a whole new world of teaching with Kevin Roughton's ideas!

—Michael Matera, Keynote speaker, International trainer, Engagement Engineer, Teacher and Bestselling Author of *Explore Like a Pirate.*

For many years in his leadership roles for Walt Disney Imagineering Disney Legend Marty Sklar shared his distillation of theme park design wisdom known as "Mickey's Ten Commandments," eventually using them as the basis for the book *One Little Spark* in which he elaborated on each commandment and provided examples (both good and bad) of each from his long history with the Disney company. As "Mickey's Ten Commandments" spread beyond the themed entertainment community, fans of Imagineering and Disney parks discovered that these commandments offered insight into nearly any type of creative endeavor, not just theme park design.

In his book *Teach with Magic*, Kevin Roughton provides an excellent example of just how widely applicable Marty's insights and "Mickey's Ten Commandments" are as he shows readers how the principles behind them can be applied to teaching and instructional design. Roughton shares examples from his years as a middle school history teacher of how he applied each of "Mickey's Ten Commandments" in his classroom to more fully engage his students. Even if you are not a teacher, there's plenty to learn from *Teach with Magic*. It will show you how to add a little Disney magic to whatever you do!

—Lou Prosperi, Author of *Tell Your Story the Walt Disney World Way*, *The Imagineering Pyramid*, and *The Imagineering Process*.

ABOUT THEME PARK PRESS

Theme Park Press publishes books primarily about the Disney company, its history, culture, films, animation, and theme parks, as well as theme parks in general.

Our authors include noted historians, animators, Imagineers, and experts in the theme park industry.

We also publish many books by first-time authors, with topics ranging from fiction to theme park guides.

And we're always looking for new talent. If you'd like to write for us, or if you're interested in the many other titles in our catalog, please visit:

www.ThemeParkPress.com

• •

Theme Park Press Newsletter

Subscribe to our free email newsletter and enjoy:

- ◆ Free book downloads and giveaways
- ◆ Access to excerpts from our many books
- ◆ Announcements of forthcoming releases
- ◆ Exclusive additional content and chapters
- ◆ And more good stuff available nowhere else

To subscribe, visit www.ThemeParkPress.com, or send email to newsletter@themeparkpress.com.

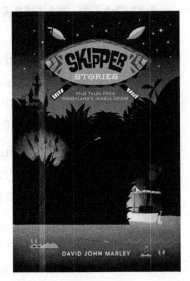

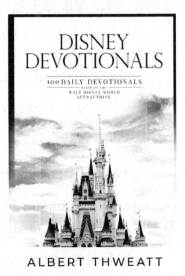

Made in the USA
Middletown, DE
12 March 2022

62526236R00119